MUSIC OF THE UNITED STATES OF AMERICA

Richard Crawford, Editor-in-Chief
James Wierzbicki, Executive Editor

---

1. Ruth Crawford: Music for Small Orchestra (1926); Suite No. 2 for Four Strings and Piano (1929)
   Edited by Judith Tick and Wayne Schneider

2. Irving Berlin: Early Songs, 1907–1914
   Edited by Charles Hamm

3. Amy Beach: Quartet For Strings (In One Movement), Op. 89
   Edited by Adrienne Fried Block

4. Daniel Read: Collected Works
   Edited by Karl Kroeger

5. The Music and Scripts of *In Dahomey*
   Edited by Thomas L. Riis

6. Timothy Swan: Psalmody and Secular Songs
   Edited by Nym Cooke

7. Harrigan and Braham: Collected Songs, 1873–1896
   Edited by Jon W. Finson

8. Lou Harrison: Selected Keyboard and Chamber Music, 1937–1994
   Edited by Leta E. Miller

9. Harry Partch: *Barstow* (1968)
   Edited by Richard Kassel

10. Thomas Wright "Fats" Waller: Performances in Transcription, 1927–1943
    Edited by Paul S. Machlin

11. Writing American Indian Music: Historic Transcriptions, Notations, and Arrangements
    Edited by Victoria Lindsay Levine

12. Charles Ives: 129 Songs
    Edited by H. Wiley Hitchcock

13. Leo Ornstein: Quintette for Piano and Strings, Op. 92
    Edited by Denise Von Glahn and Michael Broyles

14. Dudley Buck: American Victorian Choral Music
    Edited by N. Lee Orr

15. Earl "Fatha" Hines: Selected Piano Solos, 1928–1941
    Edited by Jeffrey Taylor

16. David Moritz Michael: Complete Wind Chamber Music
    Edited by Nola Reed Knouse

17. Charles Hommann: Surviving Orchestral Music
    Edited by Joanne Swenson-Eldridge

18. Virgil Thomson and Gertrude Stein: Four Saints in Three Acts
    Edited by H. Wiley Hitchcock and Charles Fussell

19. Florence Price: Symphonies nos. 1 and 3
    Edited by Rae Linda Brown and Wayne Shirley

20. Songs from "A New Circle of Voices": The Sixteenth Annual Pow-wow at UCLA
    Edited by Tara Browner

The 16th Annual UCLA Pow Wow

Saturday & Sunday
May 5th & 6th, 2001

UCLA Campus • North Athletic Field

$2.00

SONGS FROM "A NEW CIRCLE OF VOICES"

The Sixteenth Annual Pow-wow at UCLA

Edited by Tara Browner

Recent Researches in American Music • Volume 67

Music of the United States of America • Volume 20

Published for the
American Musicological Society
by

A-R Editions, Inc.
Middleton, Wisconsin

Published by A-R Editions, Inc.
8551 Research Way, Suite 180
Middleton, Wisconsin 53562

© 2009 American Musicological Society
All rights reserved. No part of this book may be reproduced or transmitted in any form by any electronic or mechanical means (including photocopying, recording, or information storage and retrieval) without permission in writing from the copyright holder.

Printed in the United States of America

ISBN-13 978-0-89579-657-8
ISBN-10 0-89579-657-0
ISSN 0147-0078

Frontispiece: Cover of program for the 2001 Pow Wow at UCLA.

Publication of this edition has been supported by a grant from the National Endowment for the Humanities, an independent federal agency.

∞ The paper in this publication meets the minimum requirements of American National Standard for Information Sciences—Permanence of Paper for Printed Library Materials, ANSI Z39-48-1992.

to Leota Axford Browner

CONTENTS

ix	FOREWORD
xi	ACKNOWLEDGMENTS
xiii	THE ROLE OF MUSICAL TRANSCRIPTION IN THE WORK OF ETHNOGRAPHY
xv	The Mechanics of Transcribing American Indian Songs
xviii	Developing a Model for an Ethnographic Musical Edition: How to "Write" a Pow-wow
xxii	Background on the Singers and the Event
xxv	Transcribing the Songs: Priorities and Processes
xxviii	PLATES
1	SONGS FROM "A NEW CIRCLE OF VOICES"
3	1–2. Two Grand Entry Songs
5	*Song for Grand Entry I*
21	*Song for Grand Entry II*
35	3. Pawnee Flag Song
40	4. Pawnee Victory Song: *Kissaka'u*
47	5. Intertribal Song
62	6. Teen Girls' Traditional Contest Song
75	7. Song for All Women's Exhibition
86	8. Teen Boys' Southern Straight Exhibition: *Dottie Tiger's Song*
94	9. Contest Song for Junior Boys Grass and Northern Traditional Dancers
114	10. Honor Song for Ben Wolf's Family
152	11. Straight Intertribal Song
180	12. Flag Song: *Wapaha Olowan*
184	13. Retreat: *Wowapi Glupapi*
221	APPARATUS
221	Sources
221	Selection Criteria
222	Transcription Method
223	Editorial Markings
227	LITERATURE CITED

FOREWORD

Music of the United States of America (MUSA), a national series of scholarly editions, was established by the American Musicological Society (AMS) in 1988. In a world where many nations have gathered their proudest musical achievements in published scholarly form, the United States has been conspicuous by its lack of a national series. Now, with the help of collaborators, the AMS presents a series that seeks to reflect the character and shape of American music making.

MUSA, planned to encompass forty volumes, is designed and overseen by the AMS Committee on the Publication of American Music (COPAM), an arm of the society's Publications Committee. The criteria foremost in determining its contents have been: (1) that the series as a whole reflect breadth and balance among eras, genres, composers, and performance media; (2) that it avoid music already available through other channels, duplicating only where new editions of available music seem essential; and (3) that works in the series be representative, chosen to reflect particular excellence or to represent notable achievements in this country's highly varied music history.

The American Musicological Society's collaborators in the national effort that has brought MUSA to fruition include the National Endowment for the Humanities in Washington, D.C., which has funded MUSA from its inception; Brown University's Music Department in Providence, Rhode Island, which provided the project's original headquarters; the University of Michigan School of Music, where, since 1993, MUSA has made its home; A-R Editions, Inc., the publisher on behalf of AMS, of the MUSA series; and the Society for American Music, which, through its representative to COPAM, has provided advice on the contents of MUSA.

Richard Crawford, Editor-in-Chief

ACKNOWLEDGMENTS

I could not have completed this edition without the help and encouragement of friends and colleagues who assisted me during the many years it took to bring it to fruition. This was a complex project, which required proposal development, funding, fieldwork, transcription, text translation, and typesetting, as well as final editorial critique and polish from MUSA editors. I will, therefore, express my gratitude to various participants in the order of their contribution.

First I would like to thank Mark Clague, who initially approached me with the idea of a MUSA edition based on a Native North American musical repertoire, worked with me to write up the proposal, and shepherded it past COPAM (the American Musicological Society's Committee on the Publication of American Music). Initial funding for fieldwork and recording, as well as payments for the musicians—the Native Thunder and Cedartree Singers—came from the UCLA Institute of American Cultures research grant program, administered by the UCLA American Indian Studies Center, directed by Hanay Geiogamah. This grant also funded my assistants who did the actual recording, Brandon Esten and Dennis Moristo.

I am especially grateful to Ben Harbert, a Ph.D. candidate in ethnomusicology at UCLA, who so beautifully reconfigured and typeset my transcriptions into something legible, and was a valuable sounding board for my ideas (as well as contributing some of his own) during the lengthy process of transferring sound to page. His work was funded by a number of grants from the UCLA Academic Senate grants program. Finally, I would like to express my appreciation for Richard Crawford's thorough reading and thoughtful critique of my essay and for MUSA executive editor James Wierzbicki's help to the finish line.

THE ROLE OF MUSICAL TRANSCRIPTION IN THE WORK OF ETHNOGRAPHY

Creating critical editions of musical works is a long-standing tradition in the discipline of historical musicology. Such editions serve not only as keys to a better understanding of musical nuance and era-specific performance practices, but also as bridges between scholars and performers of works in the Western tradition. Because the central objects of study in musicology are the works of composers, traditionally circulated in score form, these scores are the essential documents of the discipline. Critical editions—as compared to facsimiles—are the result of careful study and interpretation of a composer's original score as well as performance practices common to the work's era; they are printed in modern staff notation, and they often include extensive notes on historical performance context. For historical musicologists, because the notes are already on a page, critical editing of someone else's score—and not one's own—is the central task of edition-making. In contrast, ethnomusicologists rarely deal with pre-existing musical scores. By and large, ethnographically derived scores are created by the ethnographers themselves through transcribing field recordings onto paper, or through transnotation from a work's original notational system into Western staff notation. This means that ethnomusicologists have a fundamentally different relationship with the score because, with few exceptions, they have in fact produced it, and often what ends up on the page is as much the result of the transcriber's musical aesthetic as it is the originating musician's. For most ethnomusicologists, the act of transcription is fundamental to the interpretive work of the discipline. Indeed, ethnomusicological transcription is one of the primary tools used in analyzing music in order to better understand its structural elements and cultural meaning.[1]

Of the three modes of scholarly musical interpretation listed above—critical editing, transnotation, and transcription—the latter two are the most commonly used by contemporary ethnomusicologists, whereas critical editing of pre-existing scores is almost exclusive to historical musicology. The practice of making scholarly editions of works has never really been embraced by ethnomusicology, because ethnographic study of music is generally centered on culture rather than on works or composers. In fact, the concept of a "work" itself is unfamiliar to the field, although some traditions, such as the art music of India or Japan, do have schools of performance amenable to compiling critical scores based upon the teachings of a master musician.

---

1. In addition to being a research method, transcription is also a practical technique with which to mine oral traditions for songs that could be arranged for amateur performance. See Richard Crawford, *America's Musical Life: A History* (New York: W.W. Norton & Company, 2001), 403 and 439.

According to Ter Ellingson, transcription, which he defines as "the writing of musical sounds," has, due to a "changing emphasis in ethnomusicological theory and method . . . declined in importance, or even become a peripheral or anachronistic remnant of outmoded ideas and methods."[2] There are two primary reasons for this perception. First, many ethnomusicologists subscribe to the tenet that to impose Western notation on non-Western music is a version of musical colonization; second, with the increasing availability and dissemination of high quality recordings with texts, quite a few ethnomusicologists now think that there is no need to include transcriptions in their works when a compact disc will represent the sound for the reader.[3] A third trend is to create alternative systems of notation or transnotation, often graphic or machine-based (and thereby supposedly culturally neutral), for individual music systems. Finally, some scholars simply find no need to discuss musical sounds, and therefore have no use for musical notation in any form.

The idea that practices of ethnographic transcription should be liberated from the colonizing impulse of Western staff notation has been turned on its head by Kofi Agawu, who argues in "The Invention of African Rhythm" (referencing the work of Reverend A.M. Jones) that,

> To his credit, Jones continued to use "Western" staff notation, bar lines, time signatures, clefs, and phrase marks to render comprehensible Southern Ewe music, thus bringing the music into a sphere of discourse that is enabled by a distinguished intellectual history and undeniable institutional power. For power is what it is all about, distortions, contradictions, imperfections, and all. A postcolonial transcription, then, is not one that imprisons itself in an ostensibly "African" field of discourse—an "Afrocentric transcription," perhaps—but one that insists on playing in the premier league, on the master's ground, and in the North. An ideology of sameness must be replaced by an ideology of difference so that—somewhat paradoxically—we can gain a better view of difference.[4]

Agawu is reacting to the plethora of notational systems (most by non-Africans) created to transcribe musics of African origin, all of which have the potential to mark African musics as "Other." A further problem created by unique notational systems devised for individualized musical genres is one of accessibility, in that the effort spent learning such a system may be more trouble than it is worth. Substituting recordings for transcriptions, which is becoming more and more common in ethnomusicological publications, removes the opportunity for the writer to communicate more detailed musical information through transcriptional analysis. And while machine-based transcriptions may indeed be culturally neutral, they suffer from the same problem that plagues individualized systems, i.e., being difficult to interpret for non-specialists without expertise in that particular system to interpret. Western notation, whatever its drawbacks and limitations, remains the closest thing to a universal scheme for representing musical sounds.

A middle ground in this argument has been staked out in the last decade with the series Recent Researches in the Oral Traditions of Music, edited by Philip Bohlman for A-R Editions. Originally planned as a bridge between ethnographic transcription

---

2. Ter Ellingson, "Transcription," in *Ethnomusicology: An Introduction*, ed. Helen Myers (New York and London: W.W. Norton & Company, 1992), 110. Ellingson, an ethnomusicologist at the University of Washington, has written a number of essays on the topic of transcription, including the entry in the most recent edition of the *New Grove Dictionary of Music and Musicians*.

3. The theme for the 51st Annual Meeting of the Society for Ethnomusicology (15–19 November 2006) was "Decolonizing Ethnomusicology." The meeting featured a session titled "Decolonizing American Indian Music," which included discussion on the appropriateness of using Western notation when transcribing Native American songs. The papers in the session, however, did not really engage with the pros and cons of transcribing Native songs in Western notation, even though, according to the paper titles, they were intended to do so.

4. Kofi Agawu, "The Invention of 'African Rhythm'," *Journal of the American Musicological Society* 48, no. 2 (1995), 394–395.

and musicological critical edition-making, the basis (so far) for all the volumes in the series is music that already exists in notated form (not necessarily Western), which is then either transnotated or critically edited (if pre-existing in Western notation), using field recordings and knowledge of oral performance traditions to enhance the score. Bell Yung's *Celestial Airs of Antiquity: Music of the Seven-String Zither of China* is a good example of this approach.[5] Yung combines the original Chinese tablature notation with his own transcriptions, in Western notation, of field recordings by a famous contemporary player of the Chinese seven-stringed zither. The result is a hybrid score that documents one performer's interpretations of the tablature in a specific moment in time. But with all the volumes originating from music pre-existing in notated form, the series does not address the possibility that a critical edition might be made from music that lives entirely within an oral tradition.

The Mechanics of Transcribing American Indian Songs

In the view of some ethnomusicologists, transcription is a kind of throwback to the days before recordings were readily available and when notation literally *substituted* for sound. But in early studies of American Indian music, transcription was originally a research method that communicated to the reader some sense of what Native songs sounded like, and it was a crucial element in the work of pioneering musical ethnographers such as Theodore Baker, Alice Fletcher, and Frances Densmore.[6] For these nineteenth-century scholars, song was an important representation of the cultures they studied, for through documentation and study they could map out tribal relationships and the spread of cultural attributes from group to group. In the present day, academic students of Native American music still cut their teeth early in their training as researchers by transcribing songs from commercial and field recordings. But because prospects of actually performing songs in a community setting have become increasingly limited for non-Natives, and especially non-Native women, to transcribe a song from a recording they have made is often as close as an outsider can get to the performing opportunities taken for granted by students of other traditions. The concept of "bi-musicality," a term coined by Mantle Hood, and the related practice of participant-observation, means that ethnomusicologists in the field tend either to learn non-Western notation systems and performance practices specific to instrumental genres or to learn from oral tradition sources.[7] In many cases it is possible to find communities that not only freely allow access to musical performances by scholars but also let outsiders participate in musical activities, including religious ones.[8] American Indian

---

5. Bell Yung, ed., *Celestial Airs of Antiquity: Music of the Seven-String Zither of China*, Recent Researches in the Oral Traditions of Music 5 (Middleton, Wisc.: A-R Editions, 1997).

6. The key difference between musical ethnography and ethnomusicology is that while practitioners in both disciplines engage in fieldwork-based study of musical expression, the primary goal of an ethnographer is to document, while an ethnomusicologist also engages in interpretation of data.

7. Mantle Hood coined the phrase "bi-musicality" as a way to describe how, in his opinion, ethnomusicologists should learn to perform in the musical traditions they were studying as well as in the Western tradition. Participant observation is a form of anthropological research in whch the ethnographer literally participates in the life of the group he or she studies, usually by living in the community. Bi-musicality assumes musical competence but not necessarily deeper community connection; participant observation is not limited to musical skills, especially for those who study American Indian music, where cultural constraints limit the performance activities of outsiders. For most ethnomusicologists, however, the two research strategies are often closely linked. See Mantle Hood, "The Challenge of 'Bi-Musicality'," *Ethnomusicology* 4, no. 2 (1960), 55–59.

8. Many Native groups—most notoriously the Hopi, but also some Lakota communities—refuse to admit even members of other Indian tribes to their ceremonies, a state of affairs that began in the early 1960s, in response to the widespread use of cameras by tourists.

communities are much less tolerant toward non-Indians taking part in music-making activities, although occasionally it does happen. For the most part, ethnographic documentation of Native musical expression is through recording, not performing. And this means that the process of "getting inside" the music must happen through transcription, not participant-observation.

Victoria Lindsay Levine has edited a volume titled *Writing American Indian Music: Historic Transcriptions, Notations, and Arrangements*, for the series Music of the United States of America (MUSA), which examines trends in transcribing American Indian musics as a kind of social text and is also a detailed history of the diversity of transcription techniques and their evolution over the centuries.[9] This volume emphasizes the history of notating Native songs, but it also illustrates how little the notational toolkit used by transcribers has changed since the 1800s. Although graphs, icons, and melographs have all come into play, Western staff notation remains the dominant medium in the transcriptions, which exhibit considerable variety in their structural layouts, most of which seem related to communicating song forms to the reader. The use of staff notation and the emphasis on seeking similarities in melodic contour and formal structure makes sense given the strong links of late nineteenth-century musical ethnographers to Clark Wissler's theory of diffusionism, which relied heavily upon tracing the spread of specific cultural attributes—including musical elements—from tribe to tribe.[10] Form, scale, and melodic contour were music made concrete and measurable, not only within Wissler's theoretical parameters but within the parameters of other theoretical paradigms of that time as well, most notably Cultural Evolutionary Stages.[11]

This brings up the question of what other musical priorities figured into the transcribing of Native songs, and how they played out on the page. Charles Seeger, in his essay "Prescriptive and Descriptive Music Writing," distinguished "between a blueprint of how a specific piece of music shall be made to sound [prescriptive] and a report of how a specific performance of any music actually did sound" [descriptive].[12] At first glance, a pre-existing musical template is obviously prescriptive in this taxonomy. Yet because Seeger also considers notation in and of itself to be prescriptive, his position obscures the boundaries between ethnographic transcriptions as texts describing the music and those that are intended as guides for performers attempting to reproduce the music. Within traditional American Indian song repertoires, the lines between the prescriptive and the descriptive are further blurred, for the prescriptive version of the song is what *transcribers* create while reporting on a specific performance at literally the same moment as they are reporting on the descriptive elements. This contradiction, however, was not new to musical ethnographers when Seeger offered his

---

9. Victoria Lindsay Levine, ed., *Writing American Indian Music: Historic Transcriptions, Notations, and Arrangements*, Music of the United States of America 11 (Middleton, Wisc.: A-R Editions, 2002).

10. Diffusionism was one of the dominant theoretical paradigms of the early twentieth century in American ethnographic circles. Closely related to the German theory of *Kultur Kreise* (culture circles), it was promoted by Clark David Wissler, head curator of ethnology at the American Museum of Natural History for forty years, beginning in 1902. Although he studied with Franz Boas, Wissler believed that culture was biologically innate rather than relative. See Wissler, "General Discussion of Shamanistic and Dancing Societies," *Anthropological Papers of the American Museum of Natural History* 11, no. 12 (1916).

11. Cultural Evolutionary Stages (CES) was a popular theory from 1880 through the 1920s. Espoused by Lewis Henry Morgan, CES was a uniform model of social evolution in the form of a cultural ladder, where different societies were assigned rungs from lower to higher based upon specific cultural attributes such as agriculture and literacy. Whereas CES can be thought of as a vertical model, Diffusionism is more horizontal, because it traces the spread of various cultural elements through groups that would be assigned similar levels under the CES system. CES was used by both Alice Fletcher and Frances Densmore, not only as an organizing principle but also as a justification for collecting Native songs. By persuading composers to use them in Western Art music contexts, ethnographers were literally "pulling" the songs up the CES ladder to a higher level of civilization.

12. Charles Seeger, "Prescriptive and Descriptive Music Writing," *Musical Quarterly* 44, no. 2 (1958), 184.

famous distinction in 1958. In her 1915 essay "The Study of Indian Music," Frances Densmore discussed what was essentially the conversion of a series of descriptive transcriptions into a single unified prescriptive text, knowing full well that "Indianist" composers might draw on her transcriptions, as they had done with Baker's and Fletcher's. Densmore wrote:

> The collection of songs is followed by their transcription and analysis. There are two methods of transcribing Indian songs so that the melodies can be presented to the eye and made available for practical use. One of these methods concerns minute variations in pitch. . . . The other method, which is the one that I use, may be compared to a painting. . . . Thus if we were to study the oak we might photograph single leaves, or we might paint the tree, giving its outline and environment. . . . As one might draw the outlines of many field lilies, lay these drawings one on the other, and let the light shine through the tracings in order to observe the common outlines, so I have transcribed Indian songs and, as it were, let the light shine through the transcriptions to observe the common forms.[13]

The question Densmore posed to other ethnographers of Native music was whether or not they should transcribe a song as a specific performance or as a generalized example of a type. Her own choice was for the latter, which she called an "idealization."[14] This became the common practice in her generation of musical ethnologists who worked with Native communities. Densmore's own *Teton Sioux Music* (1918) includes a series of analytic graphs showing contours of melodies side-by-side, which were the end result of her practice of reducing songs to bare melodic outlines for comparative purposes.[15] Helen Heffron Roberts, an important figure who bridged the gap between musical ethnography and the beginnings of ethnomusicology, used Densmore as a model for much of her early work as well, writing:

> In reading over the notation, they [the songs] are not all equally clear to a musician, who must needs reduce the music to some simple formulae covering the structure, etc., in order to have them clearly in mind. . . . For the sake of obtaining a bald outline of the tune and the design which it formed, structurally, it seemed best for the time being in analyzing given songs to eliminate key signatures, musical notes, with their different values, all pitches less than whole step intervals, all measure bars and accents, all expression marks, in fact everything that might be considered to belong to the realm of color in music.[16]

An examination of Roberts's later work indicates that she backed away from creating skeletal outlines of songs, but some of the practices she lists above, such as eliminating key signatures and expression marks, gained traction among ethnographic transcribers. Even a quick perusal of Levine's volume reveals a lack of certain musically descriptive elements, such as phrasing and dynamic markings, which except for occasional accent marks are almost completely absent. Also omitted from many of the transcriptions are drum and other percussion parts. Why is so much musical detail missing from these renderings of Native American songs?

---

13. Frances Densmore, "The Study of Indian Music," *Musical Quarterly* 1, no. 2 (1915), 192–94.

14. Idealization was also the term used by composers of Western art music to described the changes they made to Native songs in order to get them to fit better within the parameters of diatonic scales, four-part harmonies, and four-bar phrases. Composers who employed this technique include Arthur Farwell (1872–1952), Ferruccio Busoni (1866–1924), and Charles Wakefield Cadman (1881–1946). Although Densmore was a proponent of using Native melodies in Western art music, by the time her work was published and disseminated the trend had already peaked. Also, her style of transcription was less amenable to idealization than that of Alice Fletcher or Natalie Curtis Burlin, an amateur ethnographer whose transcriptions were used by Busoni.

15. Frances Densmore, *Teton Sioux Music*, Bureau of American Ethnology Bulletin 61 (Washington, D.C.: Smithsonian Institution, 1918).

16. Helen H. Roberts, "New Phases in the Study of Primitive Music," *American Anthropologist* 24, no. 2 (1922), 148.

In the case of Fletcher, Densmore, Jesse Walker Fewkes, Edward Sapir, and others in the early days (1890–1930) of recording technology, the answer lies to some extent in the limits of the technology.[17] Not only could recordings only be listened to a limited number of times before being ruined, the "microphone" as such was very restricted in scope, and drum and rattle parts could rarely even be picked up on the cylinder. Although known as "field" recordings, almost all ethnographic recordings of Indians during this time were made indoors, in a controlled setting—often at someone's home on the reservation—but even then the available technologies made for uneven sound quality and bare-bones transcriptions. Densmore attempted at times to compensate for the limitations of her recording equipment by writing densely detailed ethnographic descriptions, however, because her primary aim was to transcribe melodies and map them onto graphs and tables. The absence of instrumental parts, therefore, was not problematic for her.[18]

Even after technological improvements, the practice of leaving out important musical elements continued, in large part because ethnographers tended to transcribe aspects of the songs that suited their research needs. The major analytic foci of most scholars of Native music were and are musical form, melodic contour, and overall melodic range, in large part because of the assumption that drum and rattle parts, being repetitive and seemingly similar from song to song, remain static through time. Melodic elements allow song-to-song, style-to-style, and genre-to-genre comparisons to be made. Through such comparisons, historical and intercultural trends could be mapped onto the music, which in the pre-1960 study of Native musics broke down into two broad areas of interest: diffusion of style, which was thought to mirror diffusion of culture, and change of style, which served to document historical contacts and acculturation. As theoretical paradigms changed, the priorities of transcribers shifted somewhat, so instruments (drums, rattles) are more commonly included in scores from recent decades. Yet details such as phrasing, dynamics, and articulation are still not of primary concern in musical analysis of Native songs, again because they are either thought of as similar from genre to genre or not illustrative of any particular cultural attributes. In the present day, as recordings become more widely available in tandem with published works, many authors assume that listeners can hear these facets for themselves. For those unfamiliar with Native musics, however, following bare transcriptions of many Native styles—including contemporary pow-wow singing—can be difficult, due to the complexity of the melodic lines.

Developing a Model for an Ethnographic Musical Edition: How to "Write" a Pow-wow

When first asked to consider editing a volume for MUSA on pow-wow singing, I not only had to imagine how to do something that had never before been done—namely, to make a critical musical edition based upon an event that I would record and transcribe myself—but I also had to create a format that would make the volume more than just another exercise in transcription. The attraction of a MUSA volume was that

---

17. Two competing recording technologies were available in the earliest days of ethnographic recording: the Edison cylinder and the Berliner disc (the forerunner to the modern LP). Edison cylinders, which were cheaper and more readily available, were made from wax, while Berliner discs were of soft aluminum. Moreover, Edison cylinders degraded every time they were played; Berliner discs were more durable, and in general their recording quality was better. In the end, both media were replaced in the field during the 1930s by the wire recorder, which was more portable and of much higher fidelity.

18. Omaha ethnologist Francis LeFlesche used double length cylinders and multiple recording machines in an attempt to bypass the problems of cylinder length, but most ethnographers working with Indians did not, most likely because of cost—the machines were priced at $400 in 1904, when Charles Fletcher Lummis raised the funds to purchase one.

it would allow me the opportunity to present every round of every song recorded and, by doing so, document thoroughly the variations and improvisations within the traditional song forms. In live performances songs modulate, vocables shift, tempos increase, and drum accents and dynamics follow a schema that spreads out over the entire performance rather than a single stanza of a song.[19] These performance practices are something that can only be documented by working through an entire song, and which can only be understood by transcribing a series of songs in related styles—it is not a project I ever had the luxury to undertake, primarily because there seemed to be no format for publishing such a series of songs.

But before the issues of transcription unique to pow-wow music are discussed, a short definition and history of the event is in order. Contemporary intertribal pow-wows are the most widespread and popular Amerindian music and dance gatherings in North America; across the United States and Canada, more than three hundred pow-wows with traditional singing and dancing are held each season (March through November). Music is central to the organization of these events; the drum figuratively and spiritually sounds their heartbeat, organizing both the physical dance spaces and the cyclical passage of time.[20] Although pow-wows are now heard in all regions of North America, the forerunners of pow-wow musical form and singing style originated on the Great Plains between 1820 and 1840, as documented in oral texts collected by ethnologists and published by Clark Wissler of the American Museum of Natural History in 1912 and 1916.[21] Since that time, the musical form has been diffused throughout the United States and Canada and in limited areas of Northern Mexico where tribal groups straddle the U.S.-Mexican border.

This dispersion occurred in two cycles, the first occurring between 1820 and 1890 during the pre-reservation era. During the first cycle, the singing tradition of the Ponca *Heluska* warrior society spread from tribe to tribe throughout the Plains and Western Great Lakes, and two regional styles, "Northern" and "Southern," began to take shape. The Northern style predominated in the northern Great Plains and the Great Lakes regions, the Southern style in Oklahoma. For the most part, the dividing line between Southern and Northern events is geographic: tribes north of Kansas (excepting the Omaha and Winnebago of Nebraska, and the Wisconsin Ho-Chunk) sing in the Northern tradition. After World War I, Indians celebrated the return of veterans with homecoming events that revitalized the old Warrior Societies and their songs. During the 1920s and '30s, the differences between Northern and Southern traditions in both vocal performance and song structure were codified as tribal peoples of the Plains reservations endured the ravages of the Dust Bowl. Reservation Indians, especially in the North, found it difficult to travel, and localization (as opposed to musical cross-fertilization) was the prevailing norm.

The second cycle of pow-wow diffusion followed World War II, when thousands of Plains Indians were "relocated" into large urban areas, most notably Denver, Minneapolis, the San Francisco Bay area, and Los Angeles and Orange counties in Southern

---

19. Pow-wow songs are repetitive, and individual songs are in stanzas known colloquially as "rounds," "push-ups," or "sets" depending on the geographical locale of the pow-wow. The singers perceive the songs as cyclic, and as a kind of mirror to the dancing, which proceeds around a circular arena.

20. At pow-wows, both the drum used for performance and those who play it while singing are referred to metonymically as a "drum." In this essay, I shall use "Drum" in reference to Drum groups and "drum" when referring to instruments, a practice now standard among most scholars who write about pow-wows. Also, I capitalize "Dance" when it means "dance event" or pow-wow, and use the lower case to invoke the physical act of dancing or a particular style of dancing. Finally, I capitalize "Pow-wow" when referring to a specific event, and use the lower case when discussing pow-wows in general.

21. Wissler's findings are somewhat problematic, in large part due to his aversion to doing fieldwork and his publication of unattributed sources as his own. Taken as a whole, however, and collated with the earlier research of Alice Fletcher and Francis LeFlesche, Wissler's work provides a usable time frame for the origins of the Ponca *Heluska* Society, whose song form is the basis for modern pow-wow styles.

California.[22] This migration set into motion a new cycle of pow-wow musical diffusion, as Indians whose tribal heritage was not from the Plains peoples—most prominently Navajos, but also Oklahoma Cherokees, Choctaws, and Chickasaws—started to adopt Plains music and dance styles as their own. With the establishment of "Indian Centers" as social gathering places for urban Indians, such venues soon became the focus of dance contests, and they began to offer classes and workshops in Plains pow-wow dancing, regalia making, and, to a lesser extent, singing.[23]

Beginning in the early 1970s, Indian students, many of them the children of relocation, formed associations on college and university campuses and sponsored pow-wows as the main focus of their yearly activities. At the University of California, Los Angeles, where I was to document the event for this edition, the first pow-wow was held in 1985. And the pow-wow has expanded slightly every year since then. The 2001 gathering that I recorded drew about two hundred dancers and seven Drums, with two invited Drums and the other five attending to compete for prize money in the singing contest (see plates 1 and 2). Because of the unique tribal mixture of Southern California, there has developed a custom of inviting both a Northern and Southern Drum to pow-wows of any size; this allowed me to record both styles within the context of a single event, in the alternating flow between Northern and Southern styles that is unique to urban pow-wows with mixed Oklahoma and Northern Plains Native populations. Other large urban pow-wows in "border" states also invite both Northern and Southern drums, but as we enter the twenty-first century a new player has moved onto the pow-wow center stage: the Casino pow-wow with prize monies so high that pow-wow performance is now a full-time job for an elite class of dancers and musicians. These contests include dances in both Northern and Southern styles as well as specialty dances such as the Smoke Dance, the Gourd Dance (non-competitive), the Women's Grass Dance, and other popular regional dances.

There are relatively few scholarly studies of the pow-wow, and even fewer that include detailed musical transcriptions of any length or analytical depth. Other than my own 2002 text, *Heartbeat of the People*, on the Northern style, only a volume by William Powers and another by Judith Vander contain appreciable numbers of pow-wow song transcriptions.[24] Transcriptions of traditional War Dance or Grass Dance songs that could be used in pow-wow contexts are also relatively rare. Others who have transcribed songs in this genre (or related genres) over the years include Alice Fletcher, Frances Densmore, David McAllester, Alan Merriam, Thomas Vennum, and Orin Hatton. Except for Vander's work, in each of these cases melody was the transcriber's primary focus, with the drum providing a secondary rhythmic accompaniment as is common to Western contexts. Yet from a Native singer's (and dancer's) standpoint, the

---

22. Relocation was a government program sponsored by the Bureau of Indian Affairs that encouraged Indians to leave reservations and rural areas and move to urban centers with promises of job training and employment. It ran sporadically from 1951 through the mid 1960s.

23. For a detailed history of the relocation era in Southern California, and the role of Indian Centers in both cultural preservation and dissemination, see Joan Weibel-Orlando, *Indian Country L.A.: Maintaining Ethnic Community in a Complex Society* (Urbana and Chicago: University of Illinois Press, 1991).

24. See Tara Browner, *Heartbeat of the People: Music and Dance of the Northern Pow-wow* (Urbana and Chicago: University of Illinois Press, 2002) for an overview and transcriptions of basic pow-wow song types, including Southern War Dance styles. William Powers's *War Dance: Plains Indian Musical Performance* (Tucson: University of Arizona Press, 1990) contains some basic presentations of Lakota songs but does not include drum parts; Judith Vander's *Songprints: The Musical Experience of Five Shoshone Women* (Urbana and Chicago: University of Illinois Press, 1988) has quite a few transcriptions of drum parts and includes a number of Shoshone and Pan-Indian pow-wow songs. Other than Alan Merriam (*Ethnomusicology of the Flathead Indians*), who included drum parts in his transcriptions of War Dance Songs, and myself, Vander is the only ethnographer to understand that drum and voice cannot be separated in a presentation that is true to Native practice, for both singing and drumming are essential to the performance.

EXAMPLE 1.   Judith Vander's marking of off-beat vocal emphases.

EXAMPLE 2.   Vander's use of arrows to show how vocal stresses fit in between drum beats.

drumbeats are the musical focal point, and singing and dancing *accompany the drum.*[25] With this aesthetic concept in mind, I have developed a model for transcription that entails using traditional Western notation both abstractly, to represent pitch, rhythm, phrasing, and dynamics, and graphically, as a way to show musical form and the passage of time and to illustrate dance footwork.

Vander's work on female Shoshone pow-wow singers and her transcriptions of their songs were a starting point for my own transcriptions in *Heartbeat of the People*. Two elements separate Vander's documentations from previously published War Dance song renderings. First, she includes drum parts and has them run throughout the entire song; second, she correctly places the vocal emphasis on the pitches that "come off the drum beat" (as singers describe it), unlike, for example, the earlier work of Alan Merriam in *Ethnomusicology of the Flathead Indians*, which has the drum beats inaccurately written as coinciding with vocal phrasing. Two musical examples will illustrate Vander's method. In example 1 she places an "x" above the pitches that are vocally emphasized by the singers, and in example 2 she positions the vocal part with arrows pointing to the gaps between the drum-beats.

Vander was, to a great extent, limited by the software (and publishing budgets) available in 1988, and the drum parts in her transcriptions are not evenly spaced in a way that graphically reflects a live performance.[26] Using the drum parts as a musical focus and layering the vocal lines over them was a technique I began to develop in the

---

25. See Browner, *Heartbeat of the People*, 87.
26. Vander wrote out all transcriptions by hand, and she did not use notation software, which would have further limited her ability for precise placement of notes. Changes in computer software for musical notation have enabled a greater precision than was available to Vander in the mid-1980s.

late 1990s, at the time when notation software had begun to allow amateur typesetters (such as myself) to attempt very precise placement of notes in rhythmic relationship to each other. Although I have notated Native music since the mid 1980s, it never occurred to me to omit any of the musical elements—such as drum parts, accents, and dynamic changes—that I knew to be fundamental to traditional Indian pow-wow dance songs. For my theoretical aim was to account for as much in Indian dance music as could be notated, and in a way faithful to the spirit of the endeavor as I had come to understand it.

This edition differs from Vander's efforts, and also from my own previous efforts, by being based entirely on transcriptions of live performances taped during fieldwork and at the same time offering these transcriptions as a unified body of song and dance from a single event. The passage of time at pow-wows is marked by song performances in a specific, codified order during "sessions" of four to five hours that always begin with a Grand Entry and end with a Flag Song and the dancers' departure from the arena. Moreover, the songs themselves follow strict musical templates, with small but meaningful variations occurring within the boundaries of the traditional forms. While the cyclic nature of the songs is mirrored in the cyclic passage of time within each dance/music session, each session's beginning and ending is marked by the dancers' entrance and exit. Although only thirteen songs from a single session were recorded, these songs cover a large range of pow-wow "doings," and they include Flag Songs, contest songs, Intertribals, and an Honor Song.[27] My initial plan was to present all the songs in this pow-wow, in the original order of their performance, and in their entirety. Here, however, I encountered difficulties with university rules pertaining to research involving "Human Subjects." To win Human Subjects exemptions required me to structure the project in advance. As a result, I was allowed to record the invited Drums, which had signed permission forms, but not those that simply showed up for the event (see plates 1 and 2). Because in the first session none of the casual Drums was asked to sing other than during intertribal dances (owing to the Arena Director's need to know which drums were suitable for specific contest songs later that evening), the result is nevertheless a fairly complete snapshot of a pow-wow session; rather than simply present isolated songs out of context, I have arranged the songs so that the reader can follow along through the session as it unfolds.

Background on the Singers and the Event

The 2001 Pow Wow at UCLA was the sixteenth annual event since 1986.[28] Founded by the UCLA American Indian Student Association (AISA) as a way to welcome to the campus Native Americans from the larger Southern California Indian community, the event was scheduled for the first weekend in May because that was one week before the Stanford Powwow, the largest spring pow-wow in California, and one or two weeks after the Arizona State University Pow Wow in Tempe and the Gathering of Nations Powwow in Albuquerque. Strategic planning of pow-wow weekends, and laying claim to that weekend in subsequent years, is of prime importance if pow-wow committees want their events to be successful. Date conflicts can rob an event of the best dancers,

---

27. The total number of songs sung during the session was twenty. Songs left out of this edition were those sung by Drums that I had not included in my original request for Human Subjects exemptions; with the pow-wow happening on a weekend, it was impossible for me to have gotten approval for an amended protocol.

28. There is a variety of spellings for the word "pow-wow," including "pow wow" and "powwow." The term is actually two linked words from the Algonquian language family, and I choose to use "pow-wow" because of spelling conventions used in Algonquian languages. The UCLA American Indian Student Association has chosen "Pow Wow" as their spelling, so I will use that terminology in reference to this specific event, and the spellings used by various pow-wow committees when discussing those events.

whereas careful placement in the circuit can attract champion dancers to campus gatherings as they travel from one larger event to the next.

Recruiting reputable Drum groups to play is also essential to an event's success, especially in an area such as Los Angeles, where the Native Californians are latecomers to the pow-wow scene and not really part of the singing and dancing tradition. Native Southern Californians have their own vibrant musical institutions of Bird Songs and Peon Game singing. Although many local reservations—especially those with casinos—hold pow-wows, participation of California Indian dancers and singers at them is virtually nil, except for Grand Entry Color Guards.[29] And although in Los Angeles there are some local Drums of reasonable quality, such as the Sooner Nation (assorted Western Oklahoma tribal members) and the Hale family Drum (Navajos who sing Northern style), the UCLA Pow Wow gains prestige in the Los Angeles Indian community by inviting and paying the expenses of out-of-state Drums with name recognition on the national pow-wow circuit. These Drum groups, who have won contests at major pow-wows, and whom champion dancers recognize as fine singers, must be contracted months in advance; they tend to be chosen through a combination of personal contacts and student preferences, which change from student cohort to cohort.

For the 2001 Pow Wow, two Head Drums—one Northern and one Southern—were invited. They were Native Thunder, from Thunder Valley, South Dakota (on the Pine Ridge Lakota Reservation), and the Cedartree Singers, a multi-tribal Southern group headquartered in Falls Church, Virginia. The Native Thunder Singers were the choice of George Patton, a Lakota graduate student who knew the group and lobbied intensely on their behalf. My first choice for the Southern Drum was the Cedartree Singers, whom I had heard a number of times at the Ann Arbor Pow Wow. Over the years I had been impressed by both their singing and their professionalism, and I had discussed the possibility of the UCLA pow-wow with the group during a meeting with them in Ann Arbor.[30] After returning from Ann Arbor in late March of 2000, I proposed the Cedartree Drum to AISA for the following year's event, and they agreed to contact Michael Rose, who runs the group's engagement schedule.

The two Drums not only sing in divergent musical traditions (Northern and Southern); they also represent two very different ways by which individual singers can come together to form Drum groups, learn and make new songs, and respond to the fickle demands of the pow-wow music consumer (primarily dancers, but also aficionados of certain singing styles, tribe-specific songs, and in some cases groups of teenage girls). Native Thunder, as a reservation-based Drum, is made up of members primarily from the same *Tiyospaye*—either through birth or marriage—who have in some cases been singing together since childhood.[31] Originally called Medicine Horse, the group was formed in 1996 by Jerome LeBeaux, and it won the Drum contest at the Oglala Nation Fair in 2000. LeBeaux leads the annual Sun Dance in the Thunder Valley, and is recognized in his community as a traditionalist. He is also fluent in the Lakota language. Yet Native Thunder makes their songs in a style known on the circuit as

---

29. Southern California tribes tend to assert their presence by making members available to perform the blessing of the pow-wow grounds, and by banning the sale of sweetgrass, sage, and sacred pipes on their lands. Sweetgrass and sage, known as "sacred herbs," and sacred pipes are not used ceremonially by Southern California tribes and are considered to be spiritually intrusive. The larger concept urges Indians to be considerate of one another's indigenous practices and not to intrude publicly upon them.

30. The students in AISA were well aware that I was planning a research project as well as sponsoring a Memorial Dance competition, and needed singers I could work with. The head singer of Native Thunder, Jerome LeBeaux, is the nephew of a friend, which facilitated my working with them through personal contact before they came to Los Angeles.

31. A *Tiyospaye* can be defined as an extended family group. Thought of as a circle of relatives rather than a clan, people are part of their *Tiyospaye* through birth, marriage, or adoption. In traditional Lakota culture, women may sit and sing with a Drum if the other singers are members of their *Tiyospaye*.

"contemporary," which in Northern parlance signifies newly created songs that stretch the boundaries of common-practice song forms and melodies. Although the group is capable of singing the required traditional songs such as Flag Songs and Retreats, most of their repertoire is made up of new Lakota songs created by LeBeaux, who favors driving rhythms closely matched to word declamation and jagged melodies with a high vocal tessitura. Like most Northern Drums, the members of Native Thunder wear athletic shirts or baggy hip-hop garb while singing. At the same time, they tend very carefully and respectfully to their performance.

The Cedartree Singers have a different kind of history. They were formed in 1992 by brothers Michael Rose and John Mark Rose (both Cherokee), who as young men had learned traditional Southern style singing from Harold Cedartree, a Cheyenne/Arapaho elder from Geary, Oklahoma.[32] The membership of the Drum is made up primarily of Native men who work in Government jobs in the Washington, D.C., area; it is multi-tribal, and even though it is a Southern Drum it includes men from Northern tribes. The members dress to perform in the most conservative Southern pow-wow sartorial tradition, with matching hats, shirts, and jackets. They sing in a manner that corresponds with their outfits, adhering strictly to the mainstream Central Oklahoma vocal style popular among the Ponca and Pawnee and carefully following the unwritten rules of song form and tempo formed by the expectations of an audience that spurns musical innovation and values the sounds of tradition. Southern Drums do not lengthen songs by adding phrases; their melodies flow from one phrase to the next with a continuity that is lacking in the newer contemporary Northern style.

Other than Flag Songs and Retreats, which Cedartree sings in a Native language (Pawnee for the UCLA Pow Wow, acceptable because one of their singers was Pawnee), their songs texts consist entirely of vocables and are thought of as intertribal and multi-purpose. The Cedartree singers make most of these songs themselves; in their one gesture to contemporary pow-wow norms, many of the songs are given formal titles that often pay tribute to the people to whom they are dedicated but which at times are more whimsical, such as "My Keen New Hat." Naming songs in this manner is somewhat out of sync with common practice in Oklahoma, where songs tend to be given tribal names if in a Native language (Ponca Song, Pawnee Song, etc.), or to be named according to their function (Contest Song, Sneak-up Song, etc.).

The Cedartree Singers have released two albums. They were featured on a CD-ROM issued by the United States Postal Service in 1996 in conjunction with the "American Indian Dances" stamp release.[33] Nevertheless, in comparison to other Southern singing groups, Cedartree has a limited repertoire, especially in the category of songs with Native language texts. What makes them stand out from the crowd (in addition to their professional demeanor) is the stunning voice of head singer Michael Rose, one of the best Southern singers on the circuit. His reputation as a singer, based upon mastery of preferred Southern vocal quality (range, timbre, rhythmic accuracy), is second to none, and it allows him entrée into the pow-wow singing community in spite of his lack of documented Cherokee heritage.[34]

---

32. In honor of Cedartree, the annual Brigham Young University Pow Wow is named the "Harold Cedartree Memorial Dance Competition."

33. Interestingly enough, almost all of the song titles on this CD-ROM (which is no longer available) are in standardized Oklahoma style, such as "The Fancy Dance Song," "Hoop Dance Song," and "Women's Southern Cloth."

34. Michael and his brother John Mark are the sons of Wilhelm Rose (German) and Princess Pale Moon (Rosa Stuntz), who claims to be Cherokee and Ojibwe but has no enrollment or documentation of heritage in either tribe. Princess Pale Moon is a controversial figure in Indian Country, and a number of mainstream Indian organizations do not accept her claims of Cherokee heritage.

Transcribing the Songs: Priorities and Processes

Foremost in my mind when starting this project was to represent Native conceptualizations of the drum/song/dance act accurately using Western notation. Pow-wow performance is fundamentally drum playing with vocal and dance accompaniment. To communicate that fact, the drum parts must be both prominent and central. This idea has led me to place vocal lines and dance parts on equal footing. Writing the melody has turned out to be a relatively straightforward task, but fixing the dance score stylistically has posed more of a challenge. Research into dance notation proved essentially fruitless, because the nature of pow-wow dancing is that of personalized improvisation over pre-set male and female footwork templates for each dance style.[35] A suggestion made to me, and one that I did investigate, was a French style of notation known as Conté, which uses a modified music staff with various symbols.[36] But this style would overcomplicate the notation of the basic footwork by adding layers of densely figured symbols for the essential dance movements while at the same time not doing justice to individual dancers' improvisational skills and perhaps distracting from the musical notation. I have settled instead on a separate dance staff on which a combination of dots and arrows signifies the movements of male and female dancers in traditional styles; these marks are lined up with the drum part to indicate the rhythm, appearing in the score as the dancers begin their movements and vanishing when these movements cease.

Dealing with form was another problem, because I had to decide whether to write out the songs with repeats and first endings or in a single long flow. Both Northern and Southern War Dance song forms grew from relatively codified binary forms, which at some point during the 1820s were stretched out by the practice of repeating the second half of the song (the "B" section) twice before cycling back to the beginning. This formal variation became known among Plains tribes as the "Omaha" style, and during the early reservation period (1890–1918) a shortened cadential pattern was spliced into the middle of the "B" phrase, dividing it into "B" and "C" phrases. Also during this era, drum accents were added at key points, codifying the Northern and Southern variations on the structural template, which was first labeled an "incomplete repetition" form by Bruno Nettl in the 1950s.[37] In bare-bones versions, each full cycle ("round") of the forms may be spelled out as follows:

Northern:
[A]   [B]   [C]
A¹ A cadence / B cadence C cadence / B cadence C cadence

Southern:
[A]   [B]   [C]
A¹ A cadence / B cadence C cadence /---/ B cadence C cadence

The dashes in the Southern spelling (above) refer to "hard beats," which are loud strikes on the drum that both separate the B and C sections and signal to dancers that they should make a bowing motion.

Because dynamics and accents were usually different after the repeat of the B/C section, which is repeated as a unit (Southern songs place three hard beats between the repeats), I decided to write out songs in their entirety, without repeat signs, which also

---

35. Dance styles seen at the 2001 UCLA pow-wow were Men's and Women's Northern Traditional, Men's and Women's Fancy, Men's Grass, Women's Jingle, Southern Straight, and Women's Southern Cloth.

36. See Ann Hutchinson Guest, *Dance Notation: The Process of Recording Movement on Paper* (New York: Dance Horizons, 1984), 88–90.

37. Bruno Nettl, *Music in Primitive Culture* (Cambridge, Mass., and London: Harvard University Press, 1956).

communicates more clearly the passing of time. Marking sections, however, was problematic because of the way songs are structured: the second occurrence of "A" is a statement of the song's main theme, while the first occurence (A¹) is an improvisation on it. In the end, rather than trying to use parts of the form as a means to mark progress points in each song, I have chosen to mark formal sections as is often done in analysis of Western scores and parts, using the letters A, B, and C to indicate constrasting and repeated sections. Some songs, such as Flag Songs, modeled on pre-1820s forms that preceded the spread of the Omaha form across the Great Plains, are simply marked A-B.

Making the scores work multi-dimensionally—as both representations of pitch and rhythm and as graphic depictions of relationships between drums, singers, and dancers—was the most difficult aspect of the project. Knowing what I wanted was one thing, but finding an associate to help me realize the notation in typeset form was another. Benjamin Harbert, an advanced graduate student in ethnomusicology at UCLA, was my partner in the final stages of the project. Here is the way he described the problems we dealt with:

> The process involved making decisions that balanced legibility (meaning a sense of the whole from viewing a part) with the exactness of rhythmic placement (to give a graphic sense of the rhythm). What is interesting about this is that grid notation would have been better for the exactness but the traditional note-heads end up being more easily digested (assuming basic literacy). I think that in addition, the unevenness of the metric organization was interestingly solved by making the number of beats even per line, although this creates other problems that paradigmatic notation would have solved, but the length of the sections would have made that layout too cumbersome. This compromise allowed for a more accurate presentation of detail (rhythm, melody and text) and overview (form).[38]

The scores published in this volume are justified by the drum parts, with the vocal lines floating above but beamed and phrased separately.

Although standard Western notation is flexible and capable of a high level of rhythmic accuracy, pitch is more problematic, primarily because the tempered scale has yet to conquer more traditional Indian songs and singers. Notions of equal temperament, almost universal in vernacular American music because of the proliferation of mass-produced musical instruments over the last century, are not fully entrenched among Northern singers, even though most of them have been exposed to the sound of the tempered scale since childhood due to the universal radio popularity of Country music in Plains Indian communities.[39]

In general, the Native Thunder singers did not sing in a tempered scale, while the Cedartree singers—with a few exceptions—did. Nevertheless, my ability to document that variation in this project was limited, not only by software but also by the knowledge that almost anyone attempting to sing from the notation in this volume would be doing so using a piano or voice conditioned by equal temperament. In the end the purpose of this edition, which is both to document this music and make it more accessible, trumped my personal desire to illustrate singing pitch in exact detail. Therefore I have limited my deviations from standard pitch to quarter-tones, while concentrating on the

---

38. Benjamin Harbert, e-mail message to author, 27 December 2007.

39. On field recordings made before the 1930s, scales are most often pentatonic but outside the context of equal temperament. The shift toward such tuning started before 1900, when missionaries with portable reed organs began teaching hymns to Native congregations. As Christian churches spread, the process accelerated, paving the way for an adoption of equal temperament even by those singing pentatonic scales across much of Native America. Kiowa and Comanche congregations in Western Oklahoma and Muscogee Creeks in Central Oklahoma who sing a cappella are an exception, with all three groups singing hymns in older pentatonic forms. Creek Church songs are in a kind of homophonic/heterophonic harmony, and occasionally wolf tones pop out of the mix when the range is over an octave.

music's rhythmic structure and vitality. The issue of temperament has piqued my interest, however. Perhaps it will lead to more study of the relationships between the spread of equal temperament and acculturation in Native musical repertoires.

During the course of this project, a number of other ethnomusicologists have asked me, quite literally, why I have undertaken it. What is the point, they have asked, of all the work involved? Why make a critical edition, and write a pow-wow out in score form? Returning to the title of this essay, I can now say that the project has taught me more about performance practices—during live performance—than I ever thought possible, and I say this after almost two decades as a dancer (and even longer as an occasional singer of women's song parts). Three fresh realizations stand out: that all dynamics (except for the rare vocal drop-off) originate from the drum; that in Southern War Dance songs, as the tempo increases during each sounding of the transitional "hard beats" (accents between the repeats of the second half of the binary), a corresponding shortening of the opening solo statement takes place; and that Northern songs in the new "contemporary" style are fashioned from a series of short phrases unrelated to the opening theme (this approach distances that style from the old "Omaha" tradition, consisting of a theme and variations that move down the scale, broken up by cadential patterns). Finally, the project has reinforced my sense that Northern pow-wow songs are rapidly changing, pushing the boundaries of the form, while Southern singers value tradition and stay firmly within it. This edition documents not only an event, but also a moment in time when the tensions between tradition and innovation on the pow-wow circuit are increasing and the split between Northern and Southern styles grows ever wider.

More than any other priority, manifesting a Native relational sensibility—in whch the past is acted out in the present through song and dance, merging past and present into a single performative moment—requires a complete telling of that story, not representations of songs without the drum or the dancers. A transcription of virtually all the elements of the drum/song/dance event in a scholarly edition is not only the closest the reader can come to experiencing the totality of pow-wow performance, but it pays proper respect to Native traditions and conceptualizations as well.

PLATE 1. The Cedartree Singers of Fall's Church, Virginia, a traditional Southern Drum. (Photographer: Tara Browner.)

PLATE 2. The Native Thunder Singers of Thunder Valley, South Dakota, a contemporary Northern Drum. (Photographer: Tara Browner.)

SONGS FROM "A NEW CIRCLE OF VOICES"

1–2. TWO GRAND ENTRY SONGS

Description.   Two Oglala Lakota Contemporary-style Grand Entry word songs, Native Thunder Singers, Pine Ridge Reservation, South Dakota. Performers are Jerome LeBeaux, Aaron Giago, Garfield Steele, Robert Brave Heart, Jenny Ghost Bear, Foster Cournoyer, Virgil Poafpybitty, Tyson Shay, Mike Carlow, and Jermaine Bell.

Date.   Recorded 5 May 2001 in Los Angeles. Transcribed March 2007.

Bibliographic source.   Previously unpublished, transcribed for this collection.

Process.   Transcribed by Tara Browner from a recorded performance of the Native Thunder Singers.

Form.   Length of Song 1 is four rounds in an A-B-B form. Song 1 segues without stopping into Song 2, which is also four rounds in A-B-B form.

Text.   Lakota language text and vocables.

Text for Song 1:

Oyate nujido
Iyokpiya tiya hiye lo
Olowan waste waci naji wa
(Wicasa waste wan iyayelo)

Our People come happily
This good song makes them dance
Everyone should come happily and dance
This song belongs to the People
(Good men go by)

Translation by Miles Whitecloud, Sioux Valley, Manitoba. Text in parentheses translated by Tara Browner.

Text for Song 2:

Waste ki lúta pe
Ake ca

The Good Red way
[sing it] again then

Translated by Tara Browner.

Tempos.   Moderate to accommodate dancers of many styles and ages, common in this type of song, with very little variation after a slight increase at the beginning of round 3 in Song 1.

Dynamics and accents.   Vocal dynamics remain at a level of *forte* throughout. As is standard with Northern Plains songs, dynamic variation is entirely within the drum part. A single player performs isolated accents, while the group renders larger changes in dynamic level.

Tonality. Song 1 begins in D-flat pentatonic (D♭, E♭, F, A♭, B♭), and seamlessly modulates for Song 2 into B-flat minor pentatonic (B♭, D♭, E♭, F, A♭).

Variation and ornamentation during performance. Melodic variations are found in the solo opening statement of each round as is usual in this style. Occasional extra-musical utterances by singers are marked with "x"-shaped note heads.

Unusual characteristics. Song 2 has the unusual melodic formation in the cadential patterns (found at the end of each section) of alternating between B♭ and C♭, rather than staying on a single pitch, which is the Lakota singing norm. Alternating pitches in cadences are standard only in Blackfeet (Blood, Peigan, Siksika) pow-wow songs.

1–2. TWO GRAND ENTRY SONGS

Song for Grand Entry I

Native Thunder

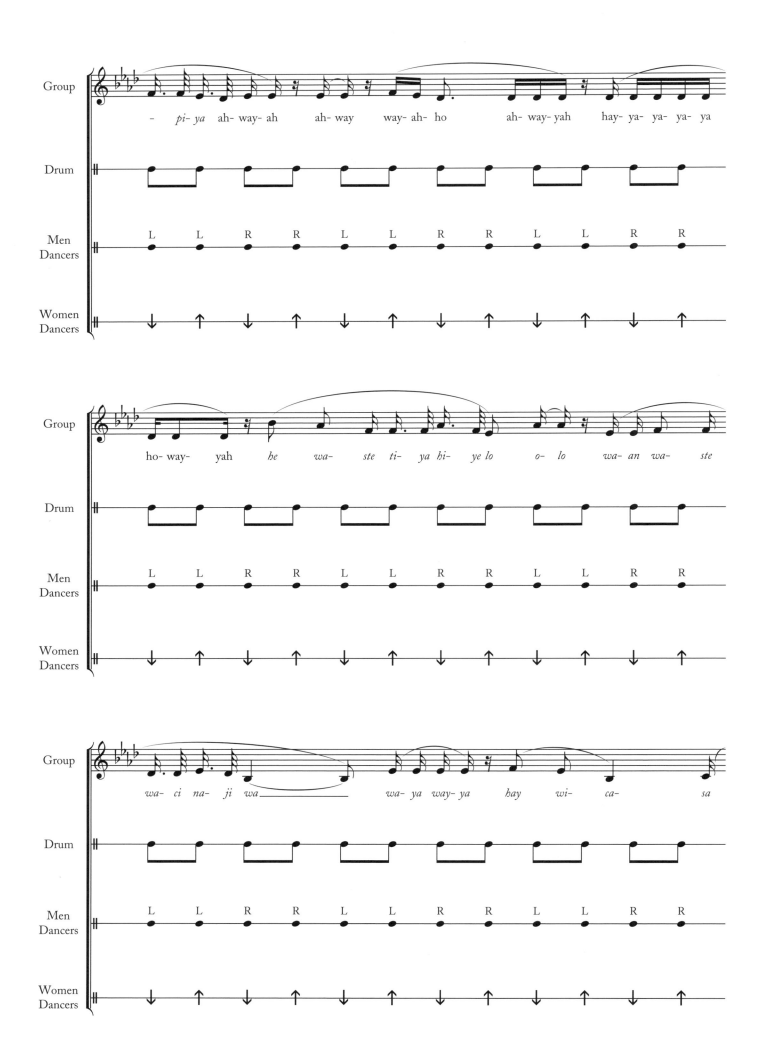

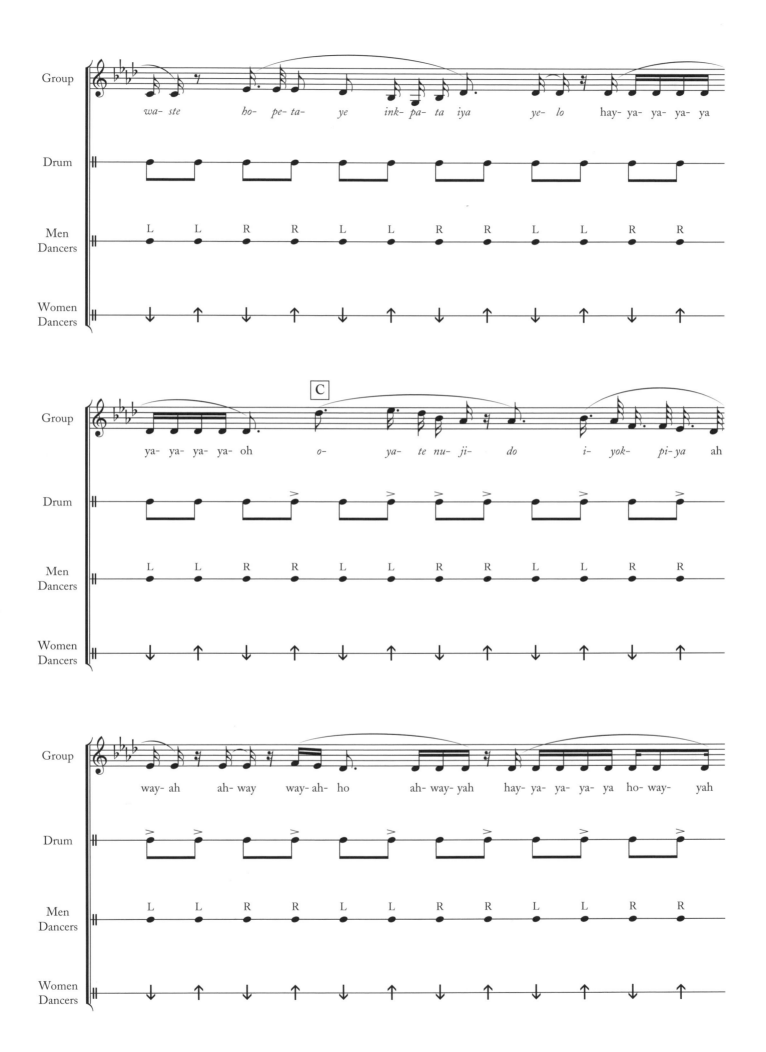

1–2. Two Grand Entry Songs

1–2. Two Grand Entry Songs

1–2. Two Grand Entry Songs

1–2. Two Grand Entry Songs

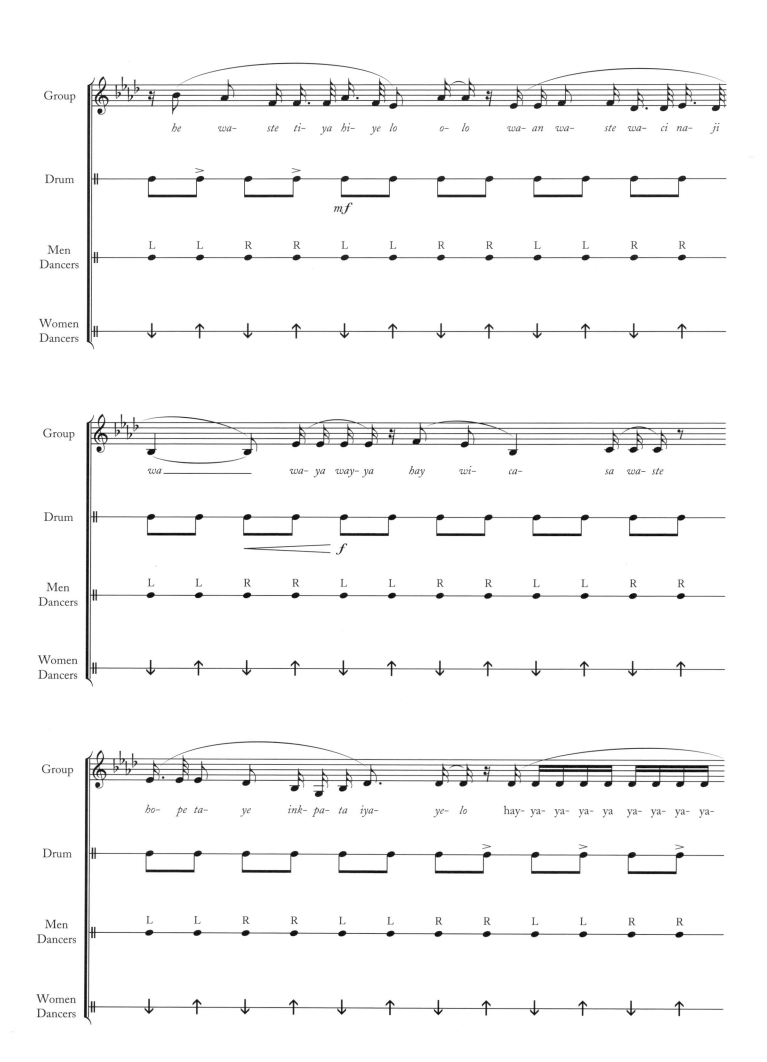

1–2. Two Grand Entry Songs

1–2. Two Grand Entry Songs

1–2. Two Grand Entry Songs

1–2. Two Grand Entry Songs

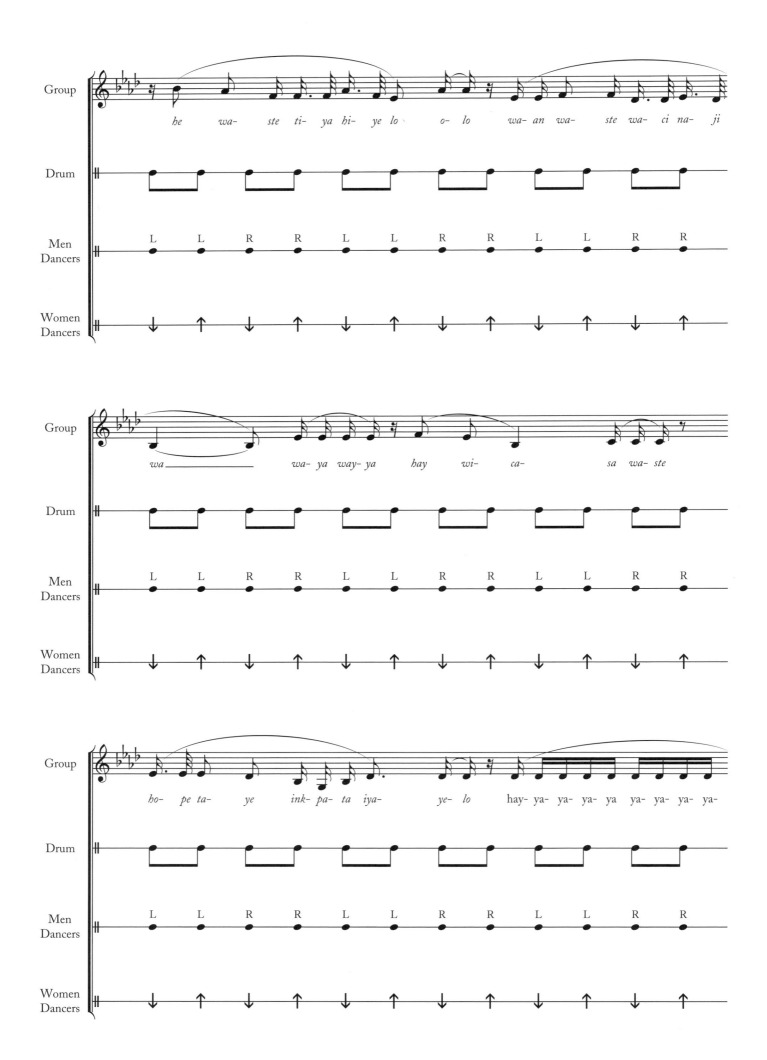

1–2. Two Grand Entry Songs

1–2. Two Grand Entry Songs

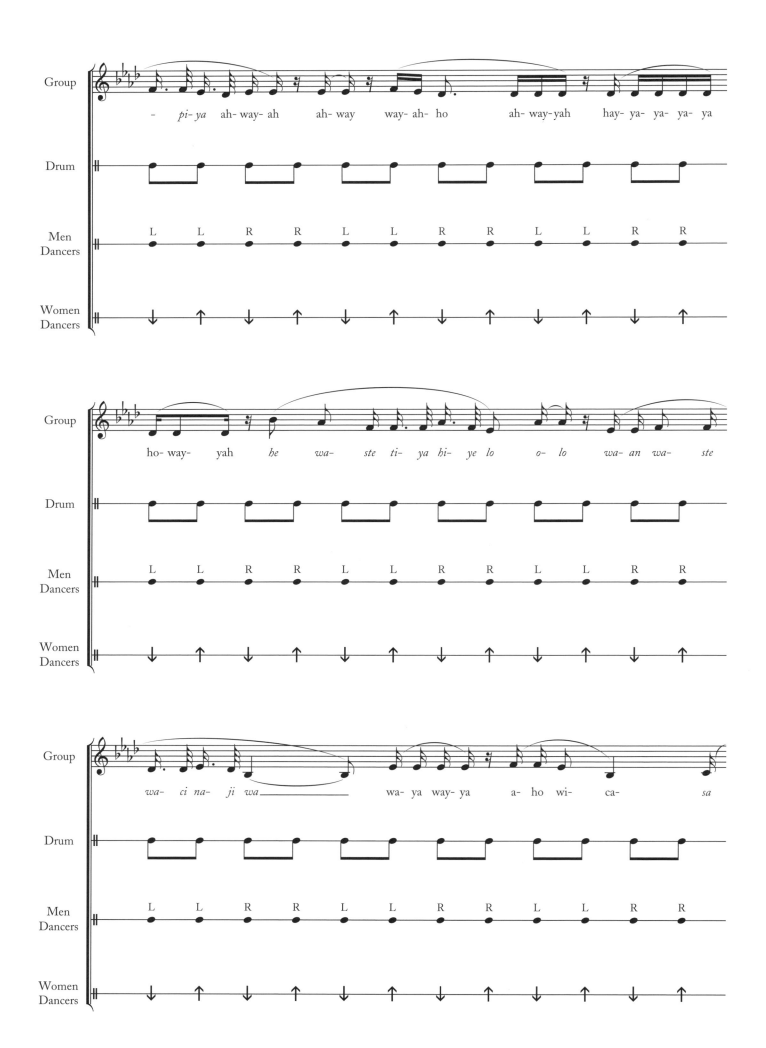
1–2. Two Grand Entry Songs

1-2. Two Grand Entry Songs

1–2. Two Grand Entry Songs

Song for Grand Entry II

1–2. Two Grand Entry Songs

1-2. Two Grand Entry Songs

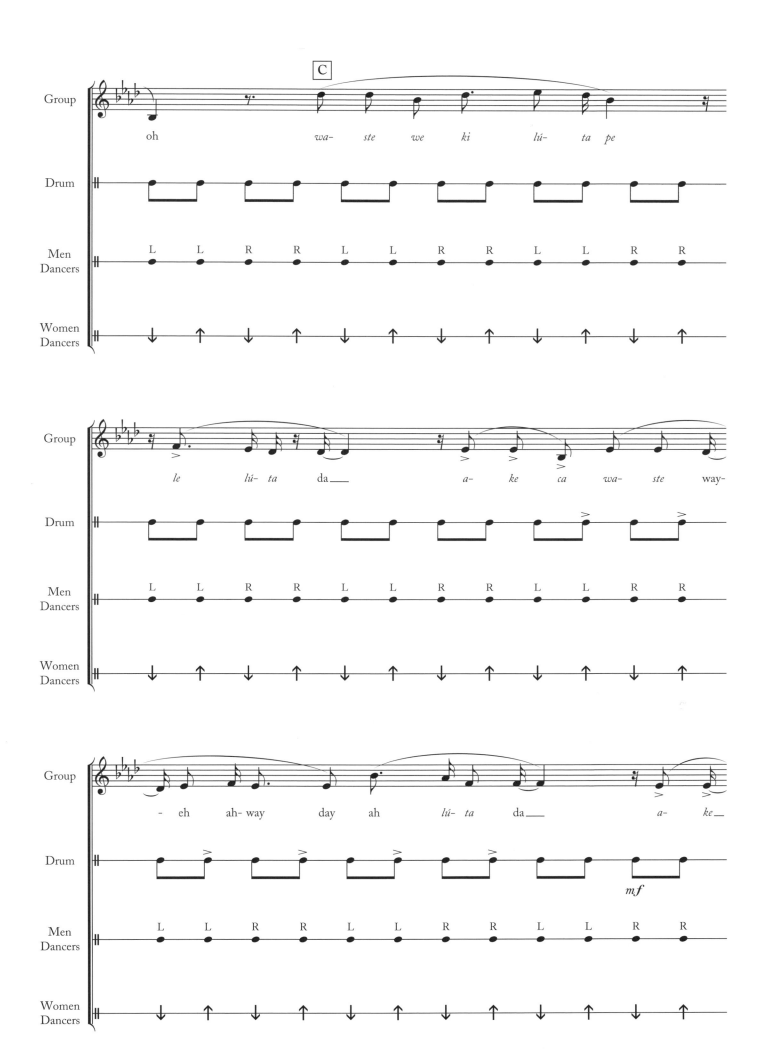

1–2. Two Grand Entry Songs

1–2. Two Grand Entry Songs

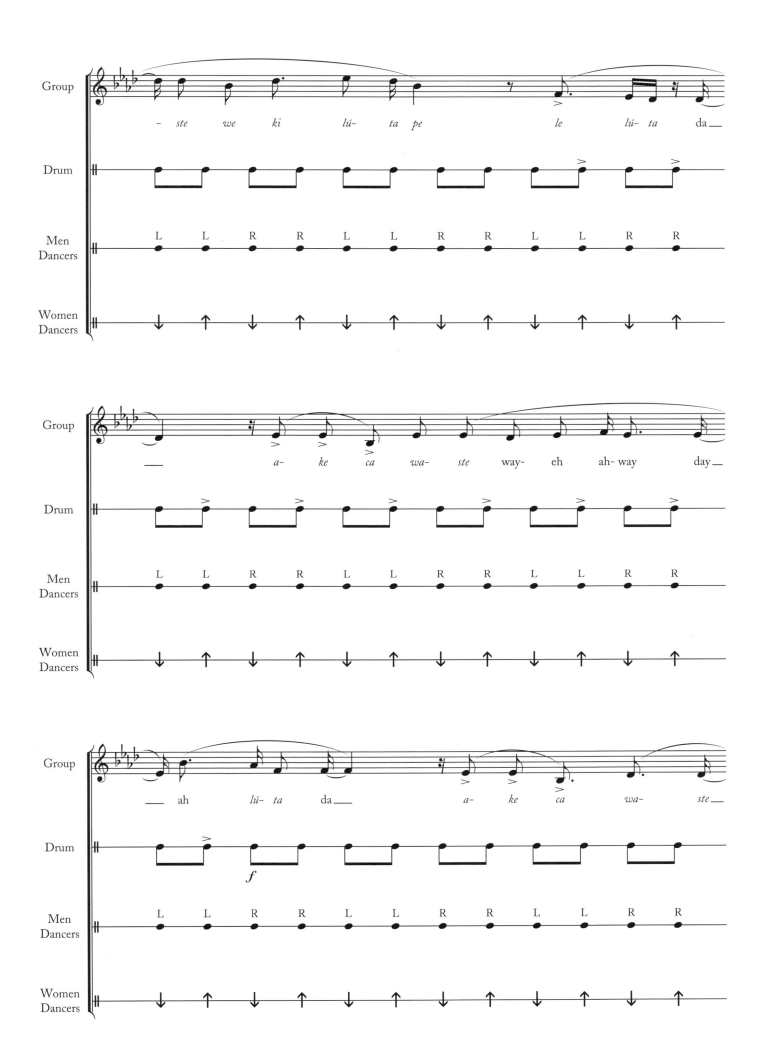

1–2. Two Grand Entry Songs

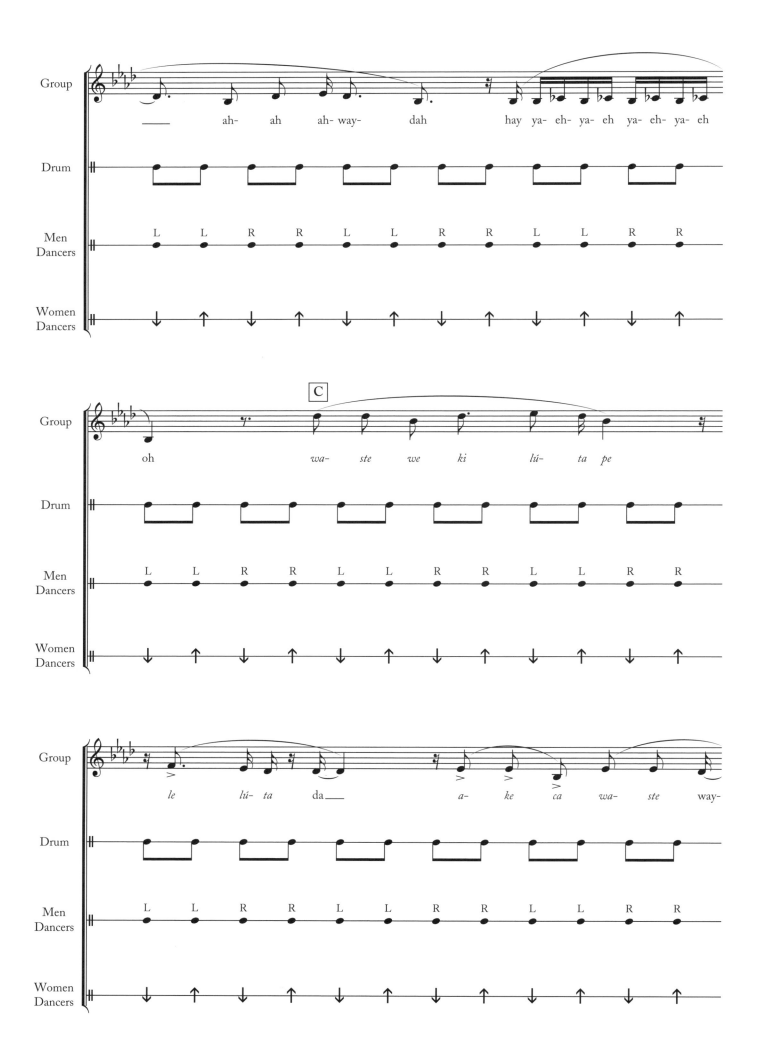

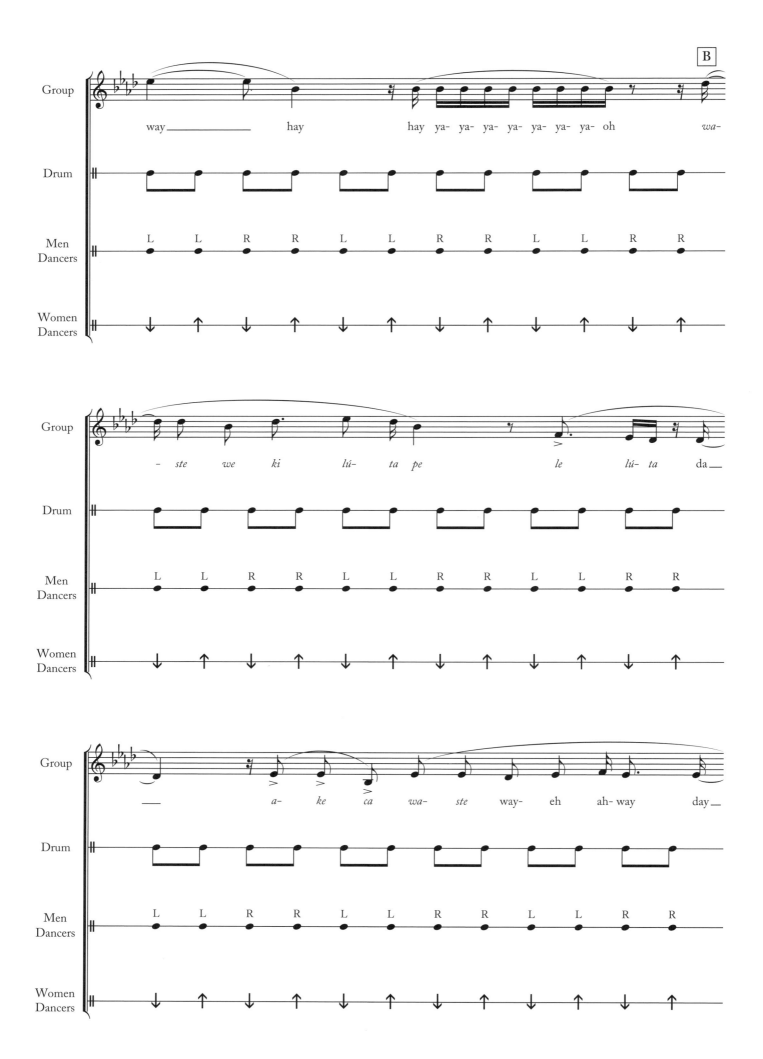

1-2. Two Grand Entry Songs

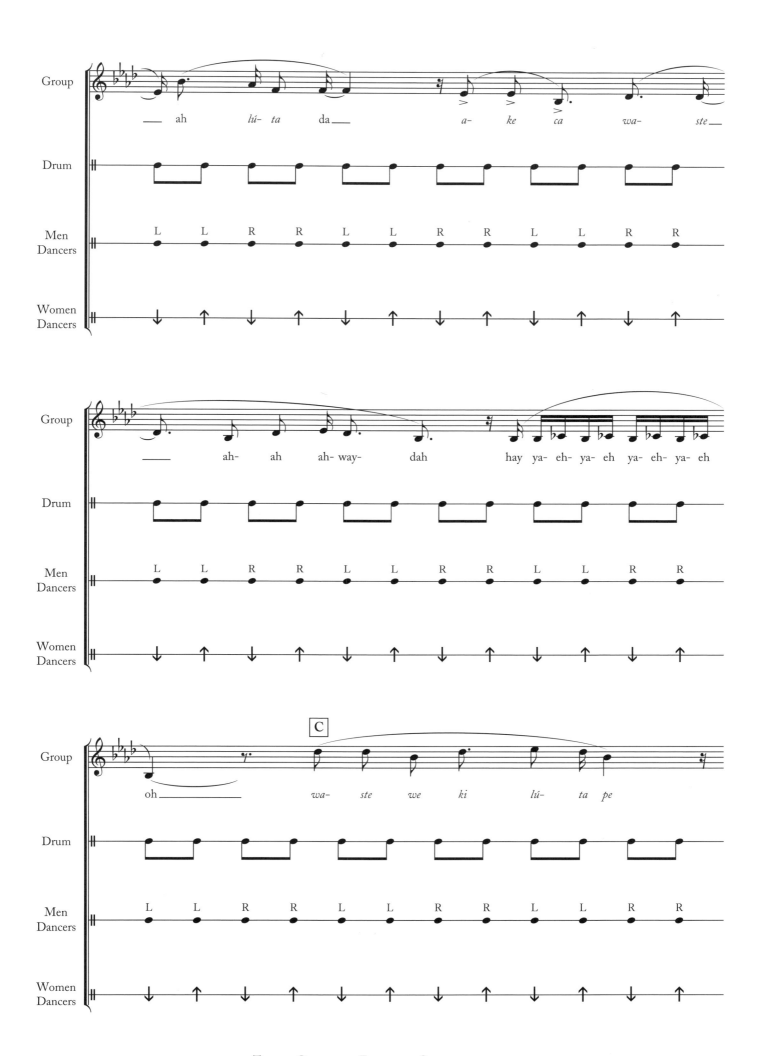
1–2. Two Grand Entry Songs

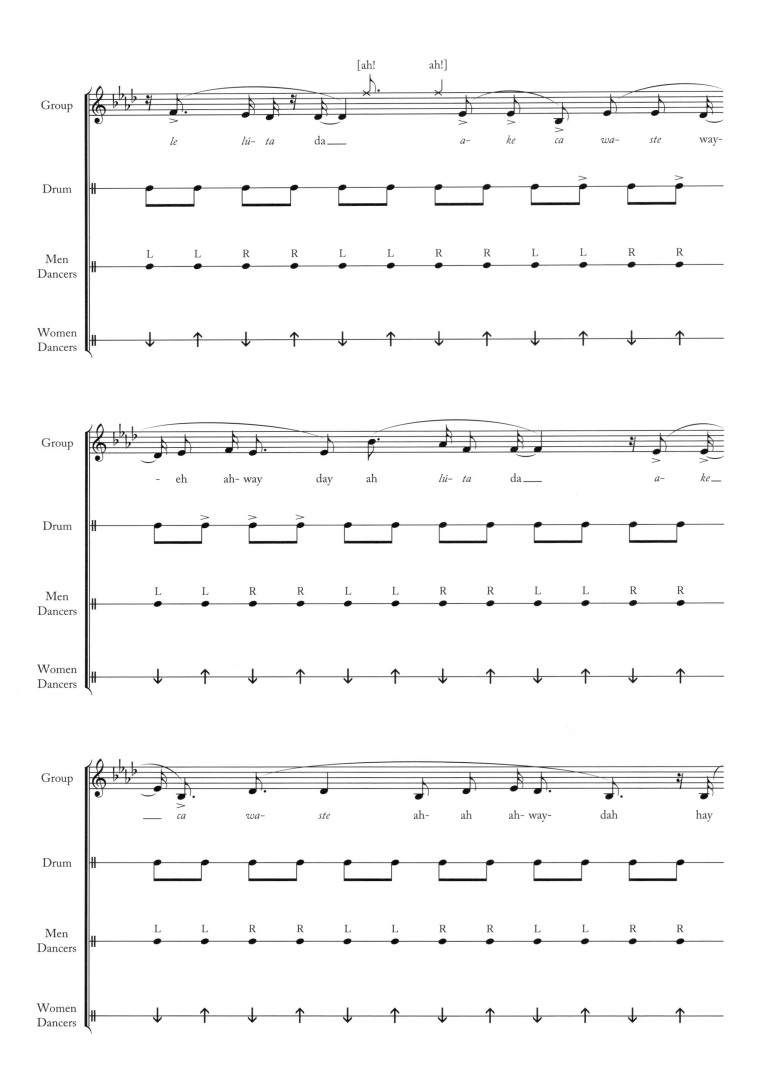

1-2. Two Grand Entry Songs

1–2. Two Grand Entry Songs

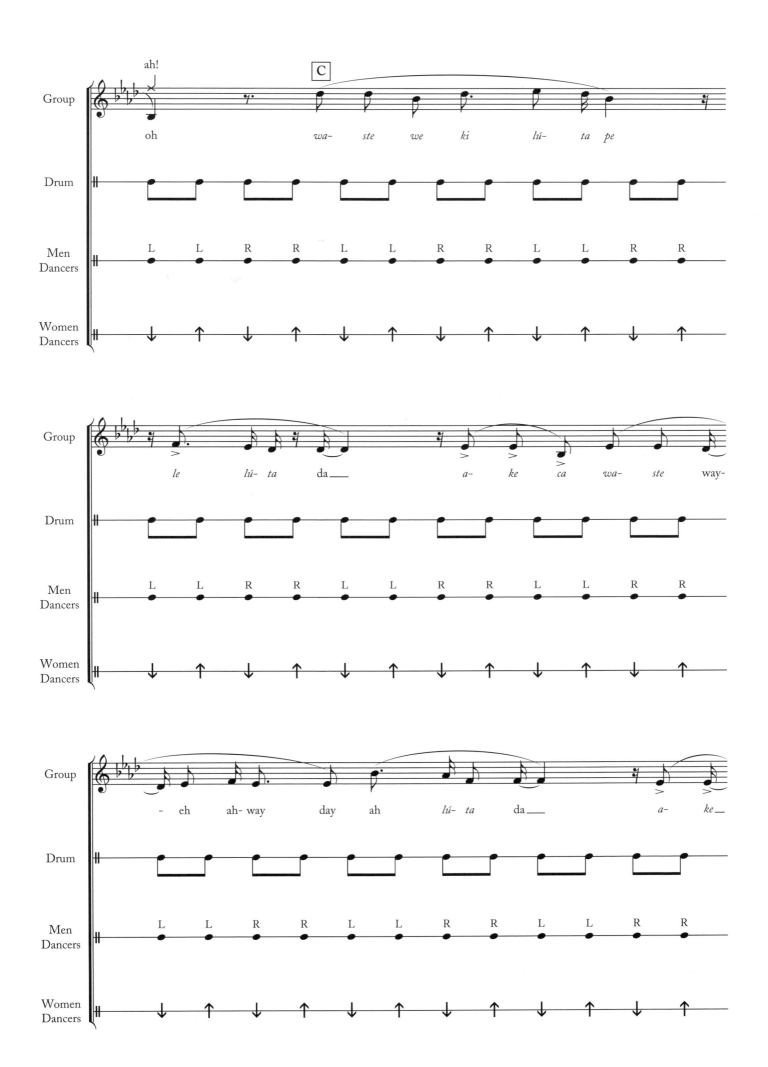

1–2. Two Grand Entry Songs

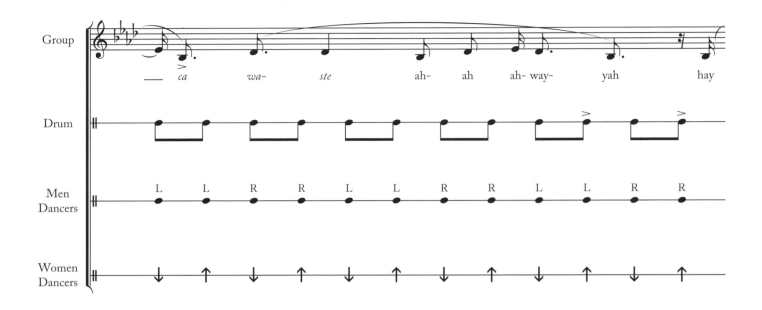
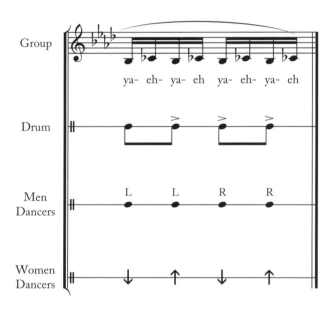

1–2. Two Grand Entry Songs

3. PAWNEE FLAG SONG

Description. Pawnee Flag Song, performed by the Cedartree Singers of Falls Church, Virginia. Performers are Michael Rose, John Mark Rose, Jeff Bailey, Erny Zah, Jody Cummings, Vernell Capitan, William A. Sebastian, William Clark, and Echohawk Neconie. This Flag Song was made by Frank Murie (Skiri Pawnee) in the years immediately following World War II. In order to sing it, a Drum should have at least one Pawnee member. Because of the Pawnee text, this song is considered a National Anthem, and may be sung before the Posting of the Colors.

Date. Recorded 5 May 2001 in Los Angeles. Transcribed August 2006.

Bibliographic source. Previously unpublished, transcribed for this collection.

Process. Transcribed by Tara Browner from a recorded performance of the Cedartree Singers.

Form. Two rounds in A-B form, with the opening statement of the theme and then two repeats by the group of the melodic motif. At the end of round 2, the drum drops out until the last two beats, when it returns.

Text. Southern plains vocables and Skiri (Skidi) Pawnee text.

This song was first recorded circa 1946, by Willard Rhodes in Pawnee, Oklahoma, as sung by Frank Murie. Translation in the Rhodes field notes is as follows:

> Translation of Flag Song made by Frank Murie, circa 1946 from field notes by Willard Rhodes, 1951/1952 (folio 3, Willard Rhodes Collection, UCLA Ethnomusicology Archive).
>
> Our Father in Heaven
> Our Boys have been fighting
> Our Father in Heaven is above us all

Rhodes, however, used a different translation for the recording that he released:

> This song was made by Frank Murie after World War II. It honors the veterans and acknowledges *Tirawa*, the Supreme Being ("He's the Boss of all things").
>
> Hail to the Flag.
> You veterans (warriors) defended us.
> God, the Father is Supreme[1]

This second translation, however, is inaccurate, because the word *Tirawa* is never sung by Murie, who instead uses the term *Ati'as*, meaning "Father" in Skiri Pawnee. My translation, based upon the performance by the Cedartree Singers, is below. It should

---

1. The notes are from informational materials written by Rhodes to accompany the album *The Southern Plains: Comanche, Cheyenne, Kiowa, Caddo, Wichita, Pawnee*, 20.

be noted that the text sung by Murie and the text sung by the Cedartree Singers is not an exact match.

hi^n-a we-si kaa-oh-ke—eh
cik-stit ti-ci ak-ku-tsa-pa-tu
ati'as tih-ki-ta-wi^n

The returning warriors/sons
carried the Flag/War Emblem well [for]
Father, the authority/ruling power

Tempos.   Moderate range for this style of song: It is in triple meter throughout. There is no dancing during Flag Songs.
Dynamics and accents.   Vocal dynamics remain at a level of *forte* throughout, and the drum is at *mezzo forte*, with no accents.
Tonality.   The song is in C pentatonic and the pitch is stable throughout.
Variation and ornamentation during performance.   None.
Unusual characteristics.   None.

3. PAWNEE FLAG SONG

Cedartree

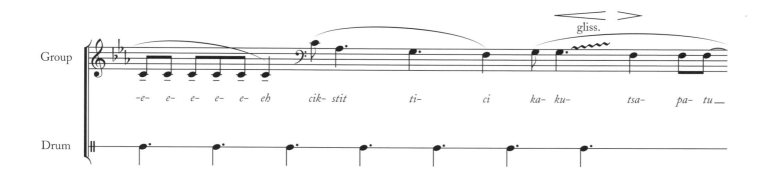
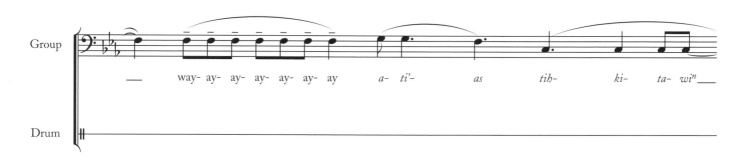
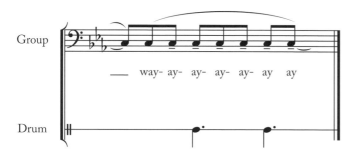

3. Pawnee Flag Song

4. PAWNEE VICTORY SONG

Kissaka'u

Description. Pawnee Victory Song, traditional, performed by the Cedartree Singers of Falls Church, Virginia. Performers are Michael Rose, John Mark Rose, Jeff Bailey, Erny Zah, Jody Cummings, Vernell Capitan, William A. Sebastian, William Clark, and Echohawk Neconie.

Date. Recorded 5 May 2001 in Los Angeles. Transcribed August 2006.

Bibliographic source. Previously unpublished, transcribed for this collection.

Process. Transcribed by Tara Browner from a recorded performance of the Cedartree Singers.

Form. Four rounds plus a tail (coda), A-B form, with hard beats between sections.

Text. Southern plains vocables and Skiri (Skidi) Pawnee text.

My translation, based upon the performance by the Cedartree Singers, is below:

ta-raa-cii
ta-raa-cii
ta-raa-cii
ta-raa-cii
ta-raa-cii
ati'as ki-wa-tu^n
aa-ka-pa-ha   sita-tiiru
taraa-cii

together
together
together
together
together
Father, the authority/ruling power
force enemy retreat/rout   they scattered them
together

Tempos. Moderate to energetic, gradually increasing as song progresses. While the male dancers dance in place, women either do not dance (Southern), or bob at the knees (Northern). There are short but dramatic increases and decreases in tempo in the transitions between the B and C sections, which is the norm in the Southern War Dance style.

Dynamics and accents. Vocal dynamics remain at a level of *forte* throughout, while the drum varies from double forte to *mezzo piano*, with scattered accents.

Tonality. The song is in F pentatonic (F, G, A, C, D), modulating to G pentatonic (G, A, B, D, E) at the beginning of the round 3.

Variation and ornamentation during performance. None.

Unusual characteristics. None.

4. PAWNEE VICTORY SONG

Kissaka'u

Cedartree

42   4. Pawnee Victory Song

4. Pawnee Victory Song

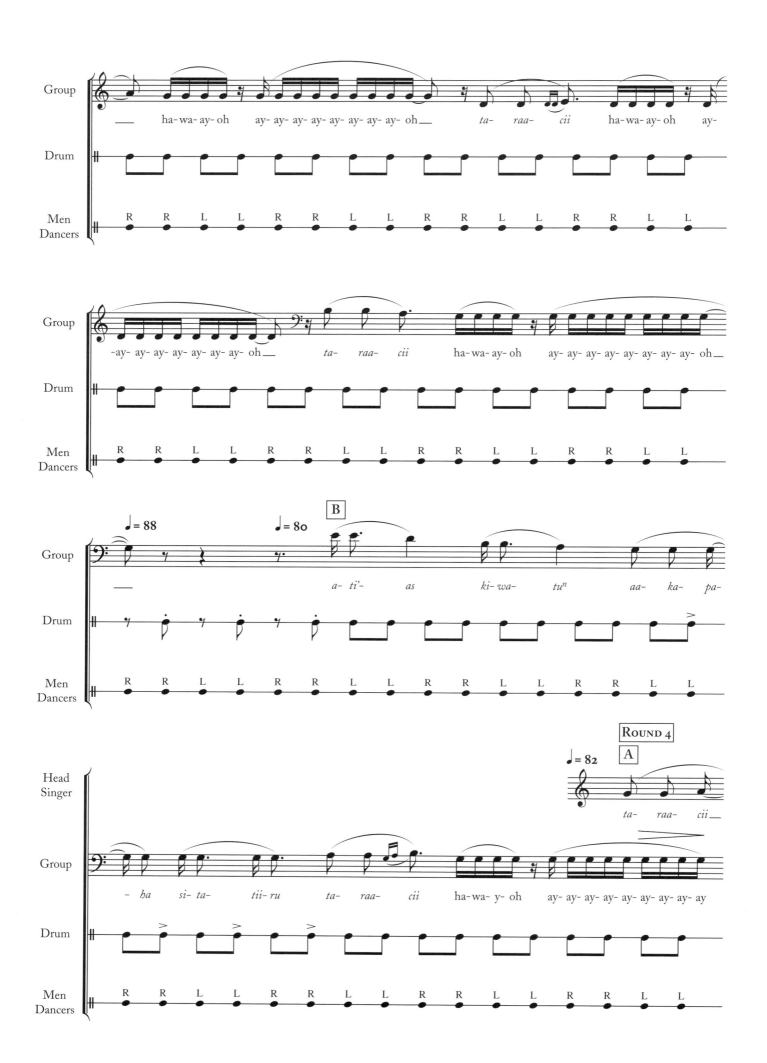

4. Pawnee Victory Song

4. Pawnee Victory Song

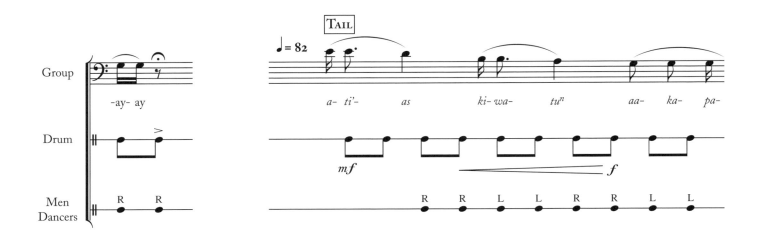
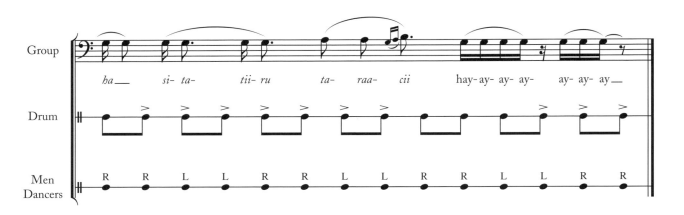

4. Pawnee Victory Song

5. INTERTRIBAL SONG

Description. Intertribal dance song in War Dance style, performed by the Cedartree Singers of Falls Church, Virginia. Performers are Michael Rose, John Mark Rose, Jeff Bailey, Erny Zah, Jody Cummings, Vernell Capitan, William A. Sebastian, William Clark, and Echohawk Neconie.

Date. Recorded 5 May 2001 in Los Angeles. Transcribed April 2007.

Bibliographic source. Previously unpublished, transcribed for this collection.

Process. Transcribed by Tara Browner from a recorded performance of the Cedartree Singers.

Form. Length of song is five rounds plus a tail (coda) in an A-B-B form, which is standard in the style.

Text. Traditional Southern plains vocables.

Tempos. Moderate range for this style of song. There is a sudden increase in tempo at the beginning of the B section in round 3, and short but dramatic increases and decreases in tempo in the transitions between the B and C sections in rounds 4 and 5, which is the norm in the Southern War Dance songs.

Dynamics and accents. Vocal dynamics remain at a level of *forte* throughout. As is standard with Southern Plains songs, dynamic variation is entirely within the drum playing. A single player performs isolated accents, while the group renders larger changes in dynamic level and hard beats in the transitions between the B and C sections.

Tonality. The song begins in G minor pentatonic (G, B♭, C, E♭, F) and modulates up to A minor pentatonic (A, C, D, F, G) in the third round.

Variation and ornamentation during performance. Rounds 3, 4, and 5 feature truncated opening statements of the theme by the head singer. This is common in later rounds in the Southern style, and ties in with the increase in tempo.

Unusual characteristics. None.

5. INTERTRIBAL SONG

Cedartree

5. Intertribal Song

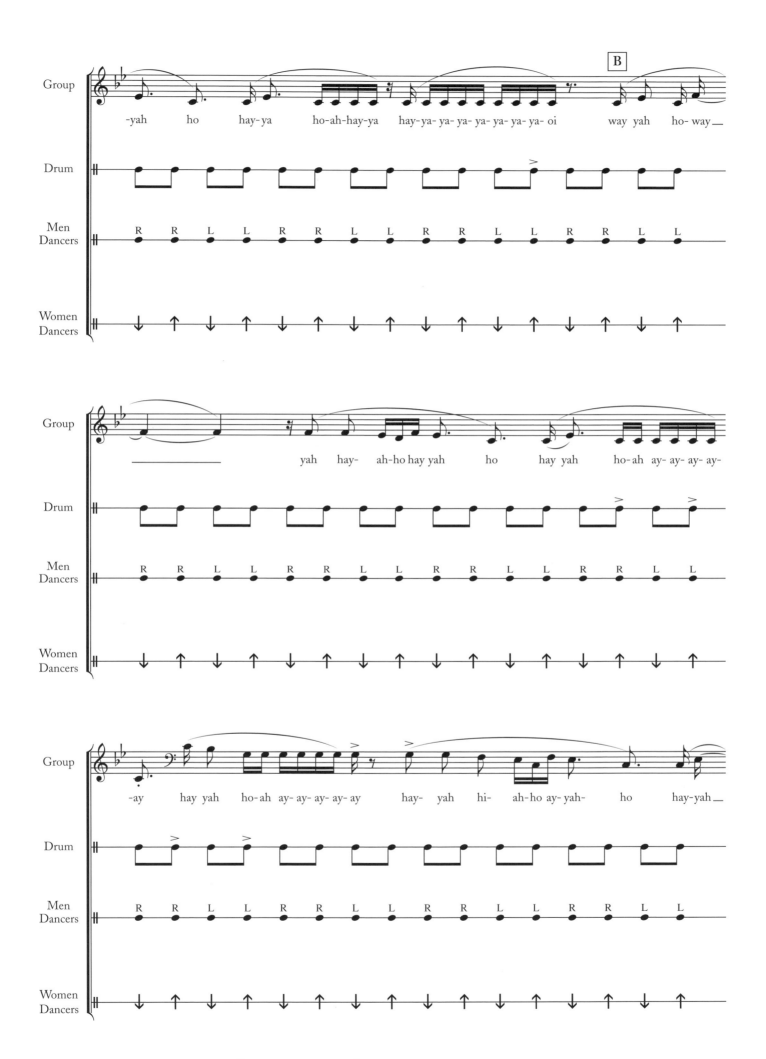

5. Intertribal Song

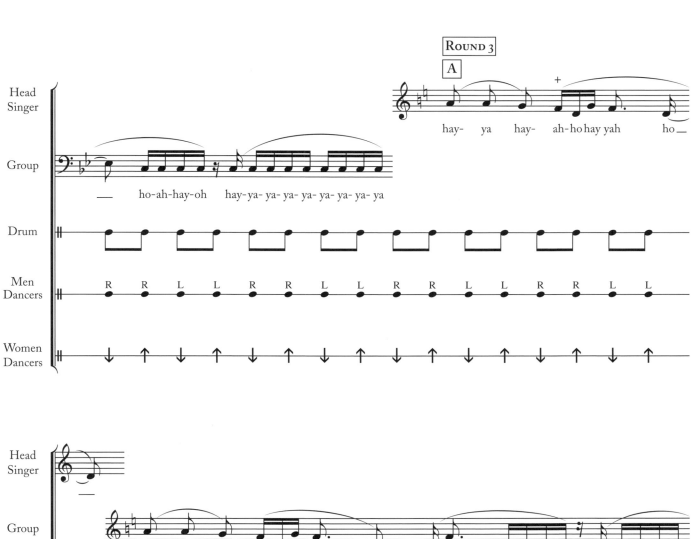
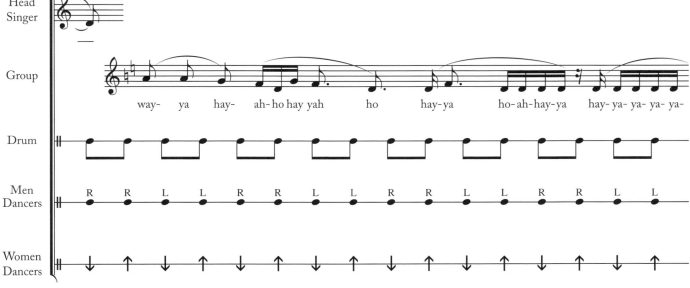
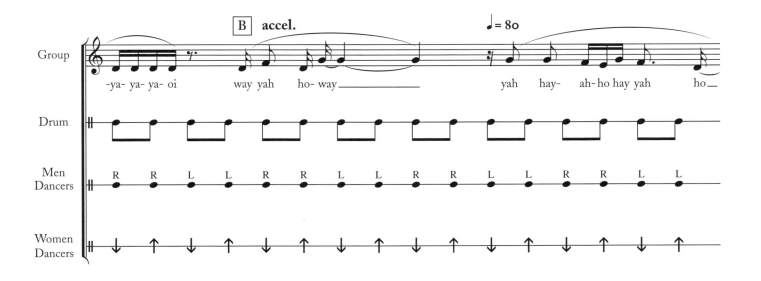

5. Intertribal Song

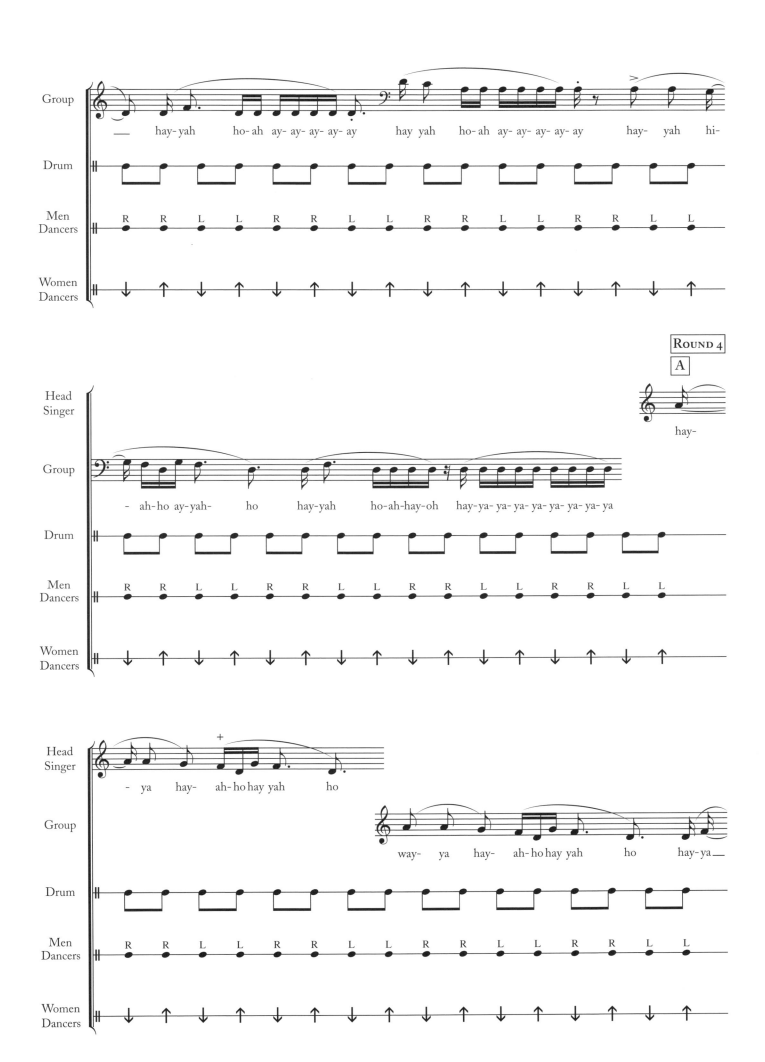

5. Intertribal Song

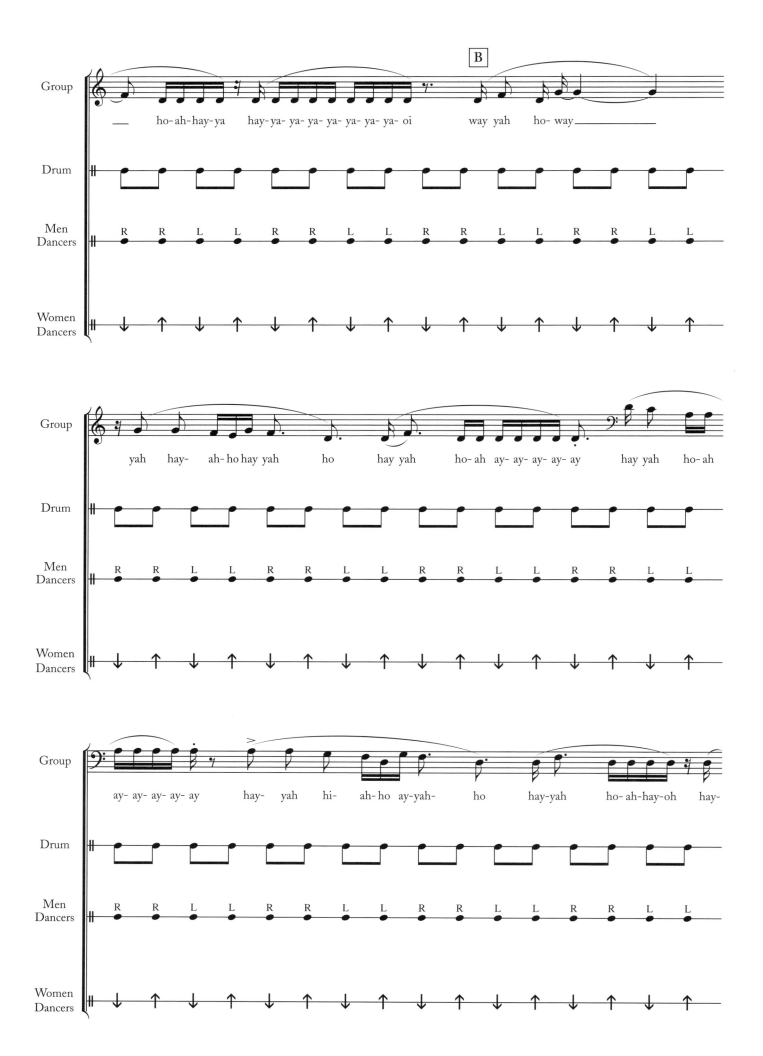

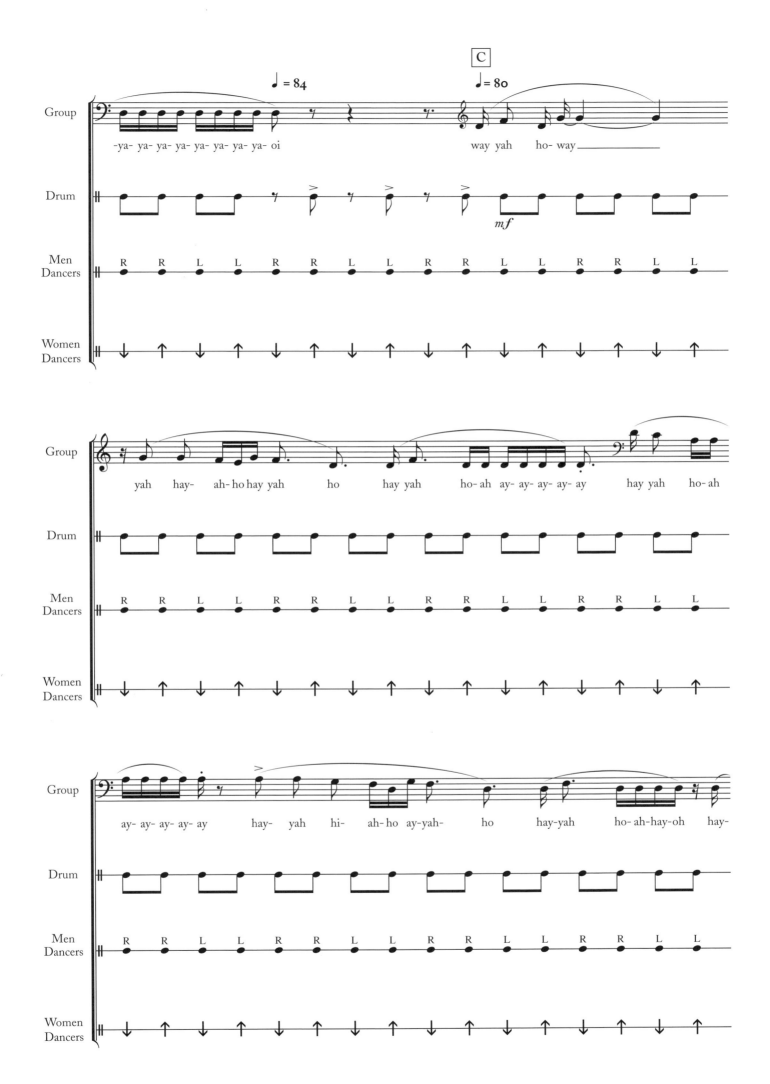

5. Intertribal Song

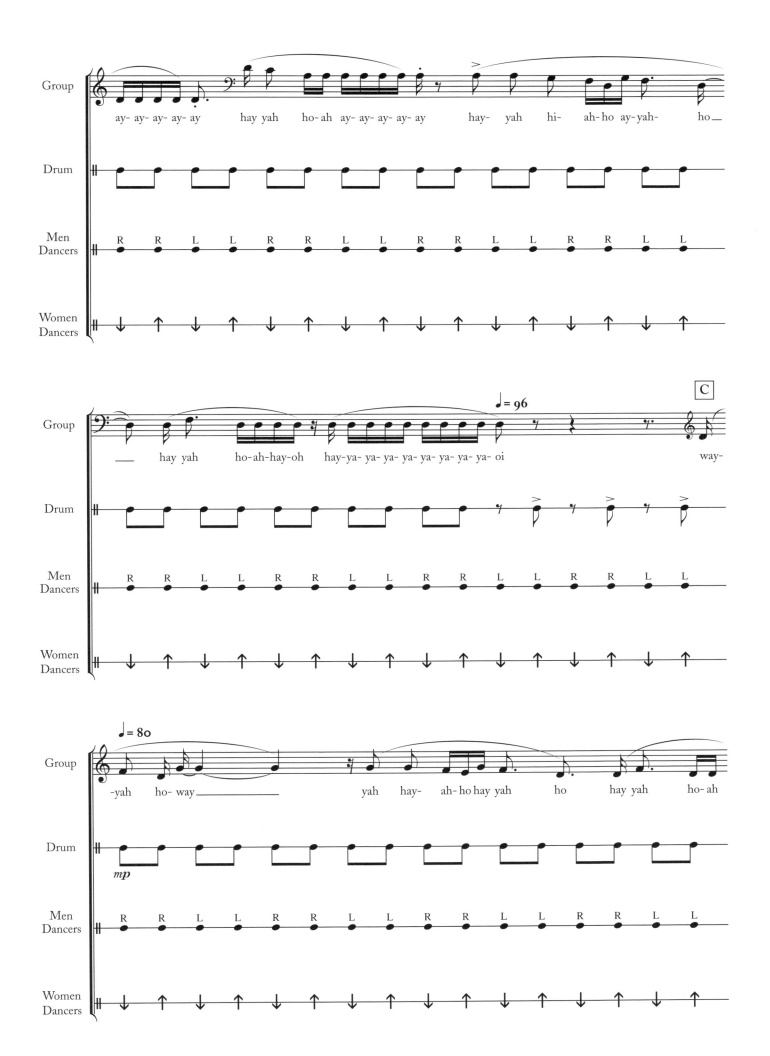

5. Intertribal Song

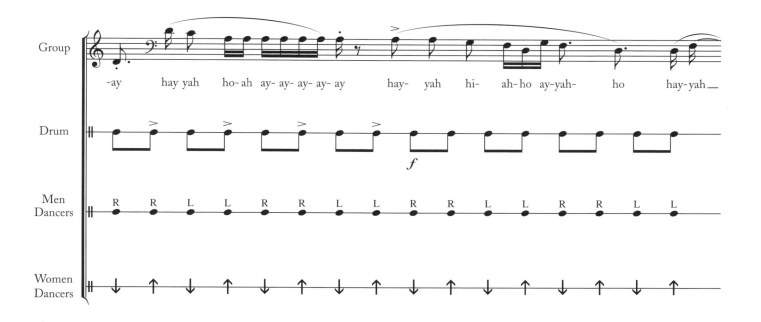
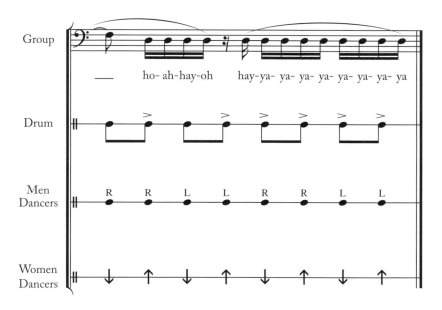

5. Intertribal Song

6. TEEN GIRLS' TRADITIONAL CONTEST SONG

Description. Song in a War Dance style, performed by the Cedartree Singers of Falls Church, Virginia. Performers are Michael Rose, John Mark Rose, Jeff Bailey, Erny Zah, Jody Cummings, Vernell Capitan, William A. Sebastian, William Clark, and Echohawk Neconie.

Date. Recorded 5 May 2001 in Los Angeles. Transcribed April 2007.

Bibliographic source. Previously unpublished, transcribed for this collection.

Process. Transcribed by Tara Browner from a recorded performance of the Cedartree Singers.

Form. Length of song is four rounds in A-B-B form, which is standard for competition songs.

Text. Traditional Southern plains vocables.

Tempos. Moderate and stable throughout the song, with the exception of short but dramatic increases and decreases in tempo in the transitions between the B and C sections in rounds 3 and 4, which is the norm in the Southern War Dance songs.

Dynamics and accents. Vocal dynamics remain at a level of *forte* throughout. As is standard with Southern Plains songs, dynamic variation is entirely within the drum playing. A single player performs isolated accents, while the group renders larger changes in dynamic level and hard beats in the transitions between the B and C sections.

Tonality. The song begins in F pentatonic (F, G, A, C, D), modulating up to G pentatonic (G, A, B, E, and D) in the third round.

Variation and ornamentation during performance. Rounds 3 and 4 feature truncated opening statements of the theme by the head singer. This is common in later rounds in the Southern style, and ties in with the increase in tempo.

Unusual characteristics. None.

6. TEEN GIRLS' TRADITIONAL CONTEST SONG

Cedartree

6. Teen Girls' Traditional Contest Song

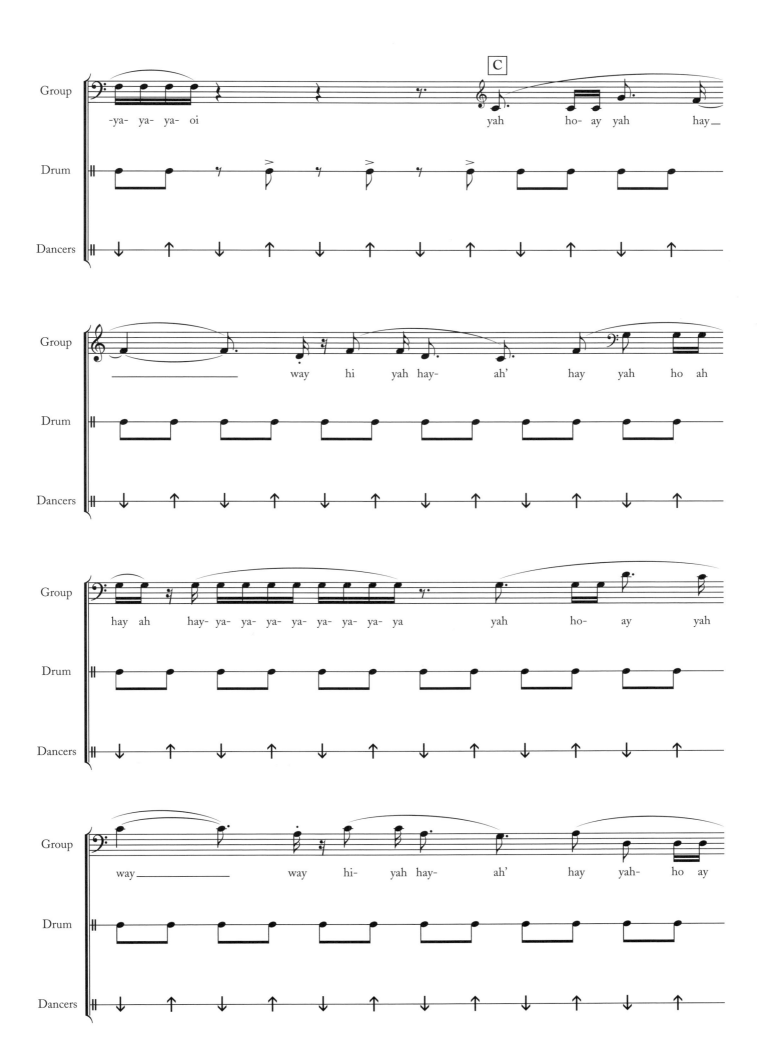

6. Teen Girls' Traditional Contest Song

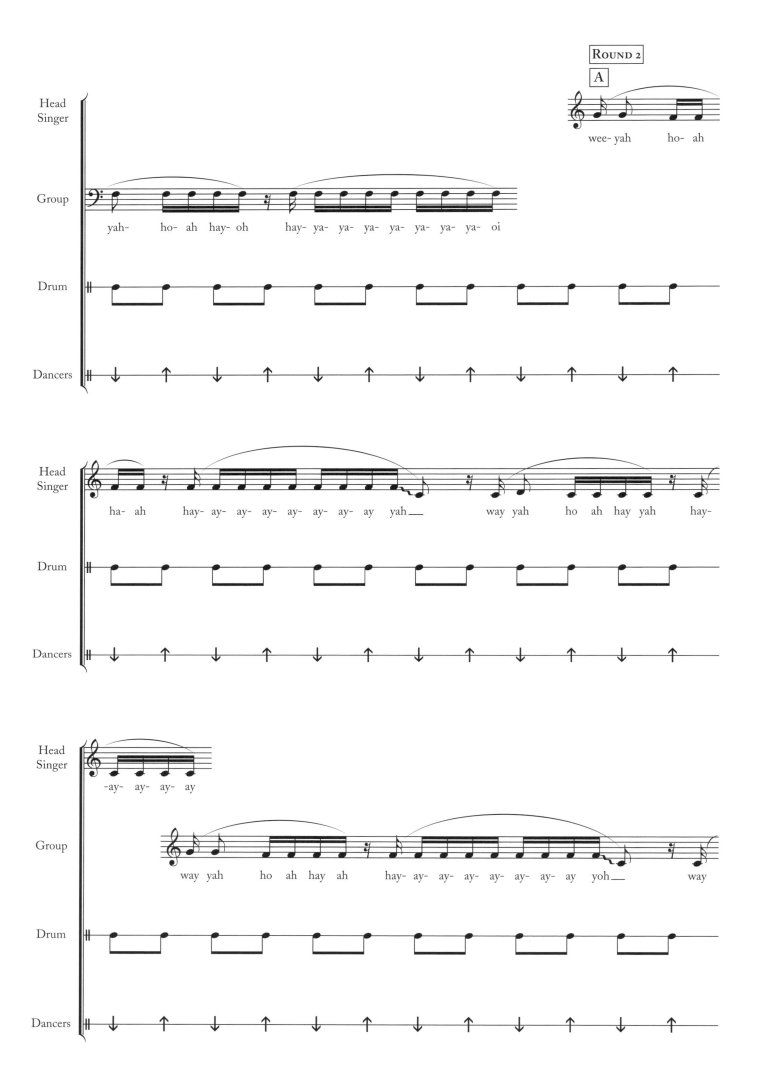

66 6. Teen Girls' Traditional Contest Song

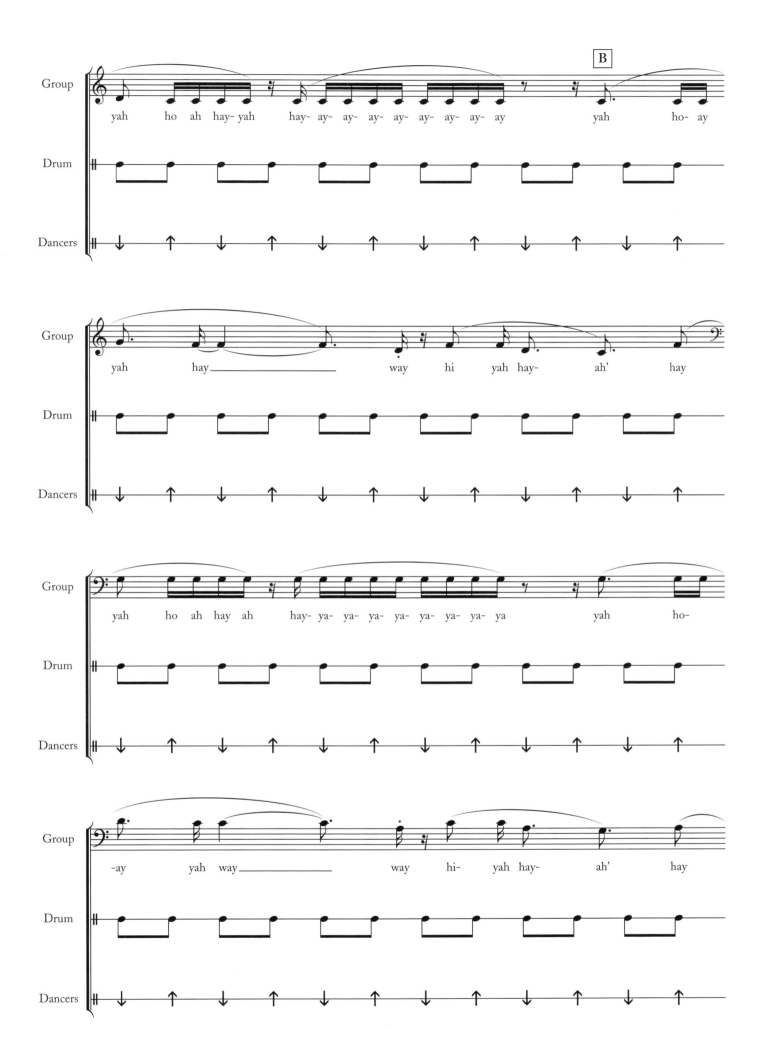

6. Teen Girls' Traditional Contest Song

6. Teen Girls' Traditional Contest Song

6. Teen Girls' Traditional Contest Song

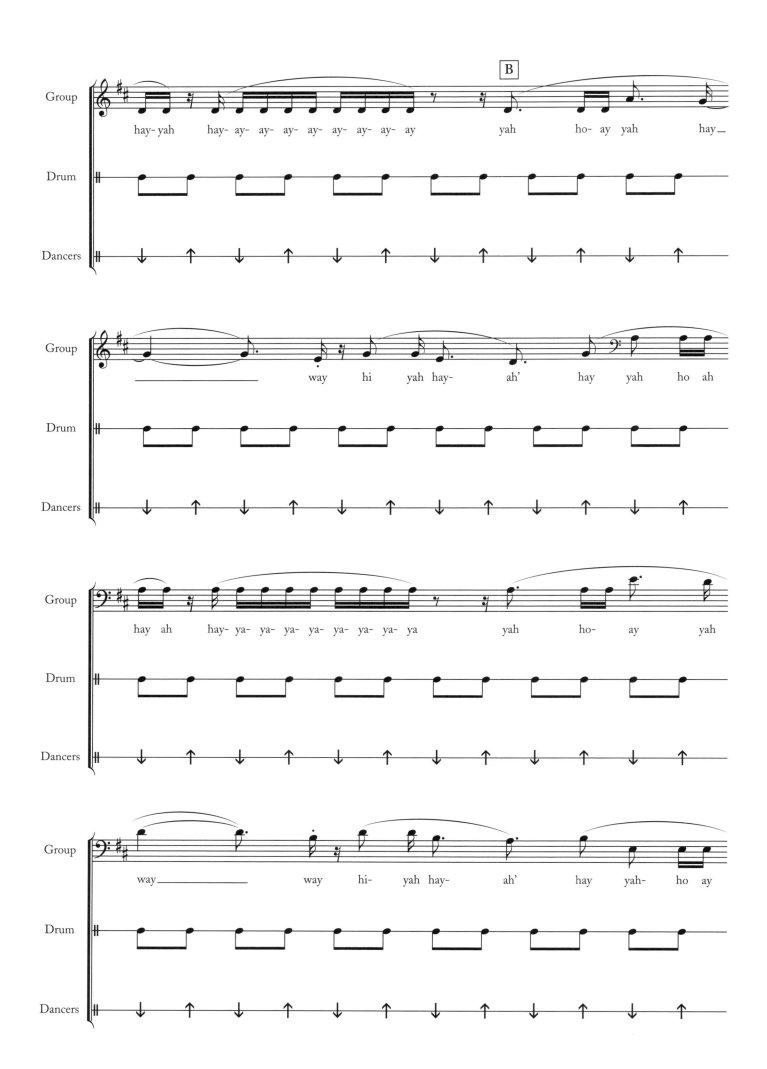

6. Teen Girls' Traditional Contest Song

6. Teen Girls' Traditional Contest Song

6. Teen Girls' Traditional Contest Song

6. Teen Girls' Traditional Contest Song

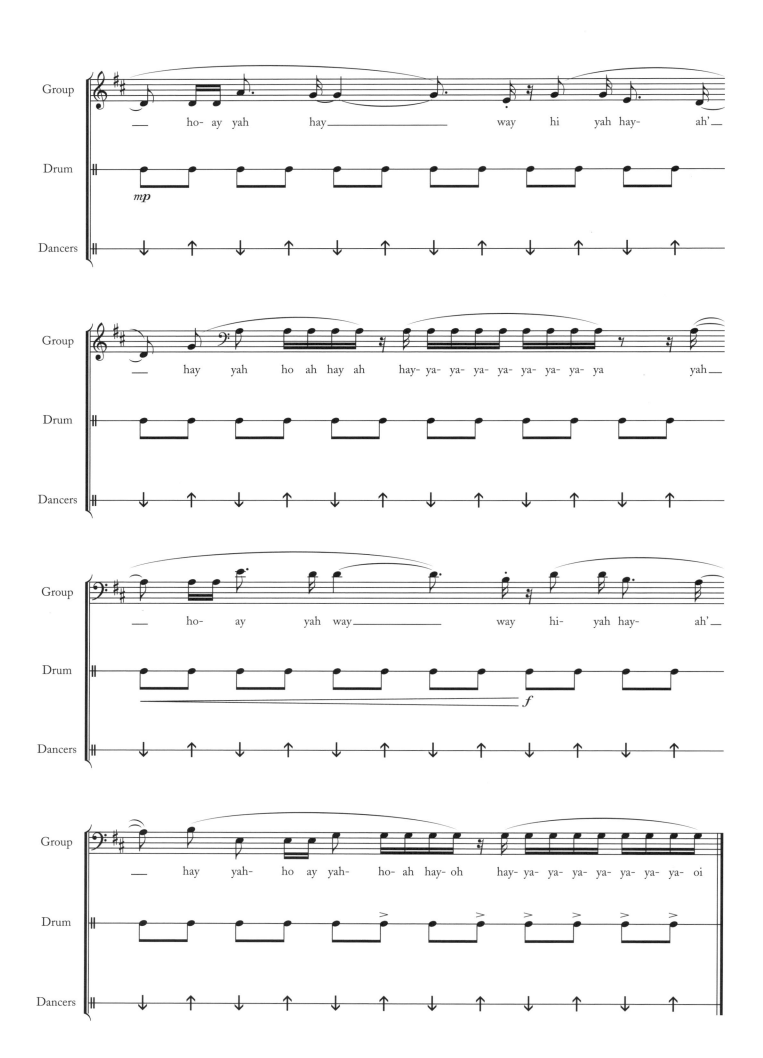

6. Teen Girls' Traditional Contest Song

7. SONG FOR ALL WOMEN'S EXHIBITION

Description. Oglala Lakota Contemporary-style straight song, Native Thunder Singers, Pine Ridge Reservation, South Dakota. Performers are Jerome LeBeaux (head), Aaron Giago, Garfield Steele, Robert Brave Heart, Jenny Ghost Bear, Foster Cournoyer, Virgil Poafpybitty, Tyson Shay, and Jermaine Bell.

Date. Recorded 5 May 2001 in Los Angeles. Transcribed May 2007.

Bibliographic source. Previously unpublished, transcribed for this collection.

Process. Transcribed by Tara Browner from a recorded performance of the Native Thunder Singers.

Form. Length of song is four rounds plus a tail (coda) in an A-B-B form, which is standard in the style.

Text. Traditional Northern plains vocables.

Tempos. Slightly faster than the norm for this style of song, but steady.

Dynamics and accents. Vocal dynamics remain at a level of *forte* throughout. As is standard with Northern Plains songs, dynamic variation is entirely within the drum part. A single player performs isolated accents, while the group renders larger changes in dynamic level.

Tonality. The song is in A-flat pentatonic (A♭, B♭, D♭, E♭, F) throughout. The D♭ is often a quarter-tone sharp (marked with a + sign), as is the F in the opening statements. There are also repeating occurrences of A♮ twelve and a half beats after B and C; in live performance these are almost unpitched shouts.

Variation and ornamentation during performance. Melodic and rhythmic variations are found in the solo opening statement of each round, and there are a number of glissandos from higher to lower between pitches.

Unusual characteristics. The series of highly articulated staccato sixteenth-note patterns in the melody, found in the B and C sections, and contrasting with long tones, are an unusual feature.

7. SONG FOR ALL WOMEN'S EXHIBITION

Native Thunder

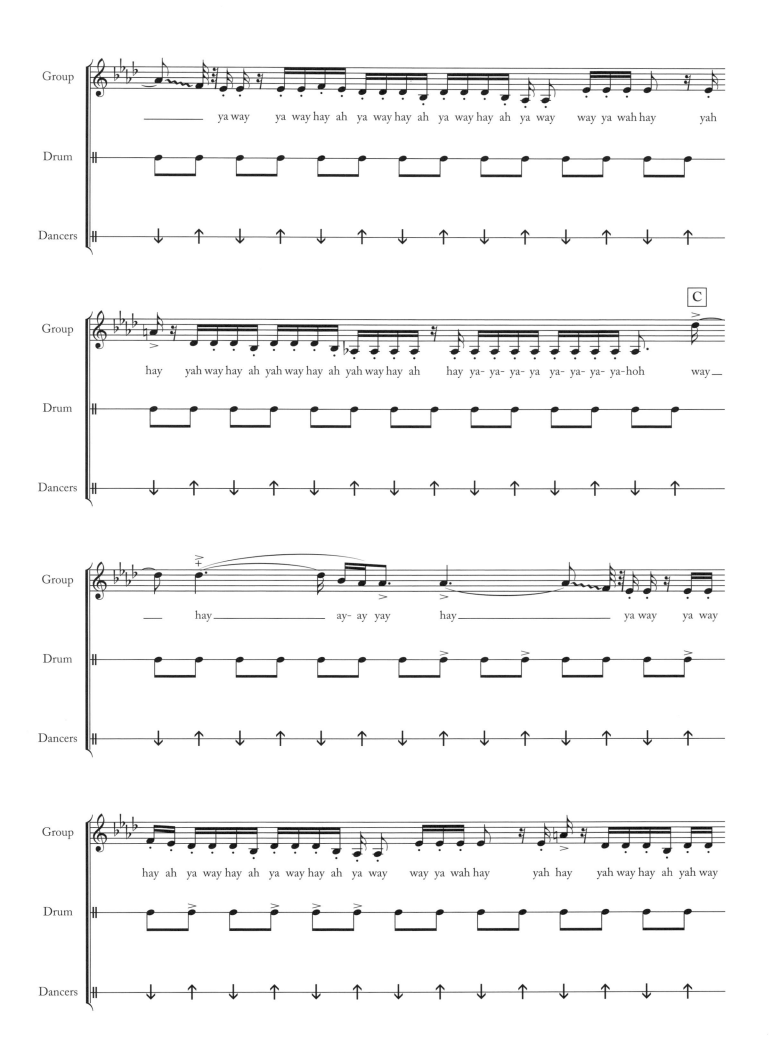
7. Song For All Women's Exhibition

7. Song For All Women's Exhibition

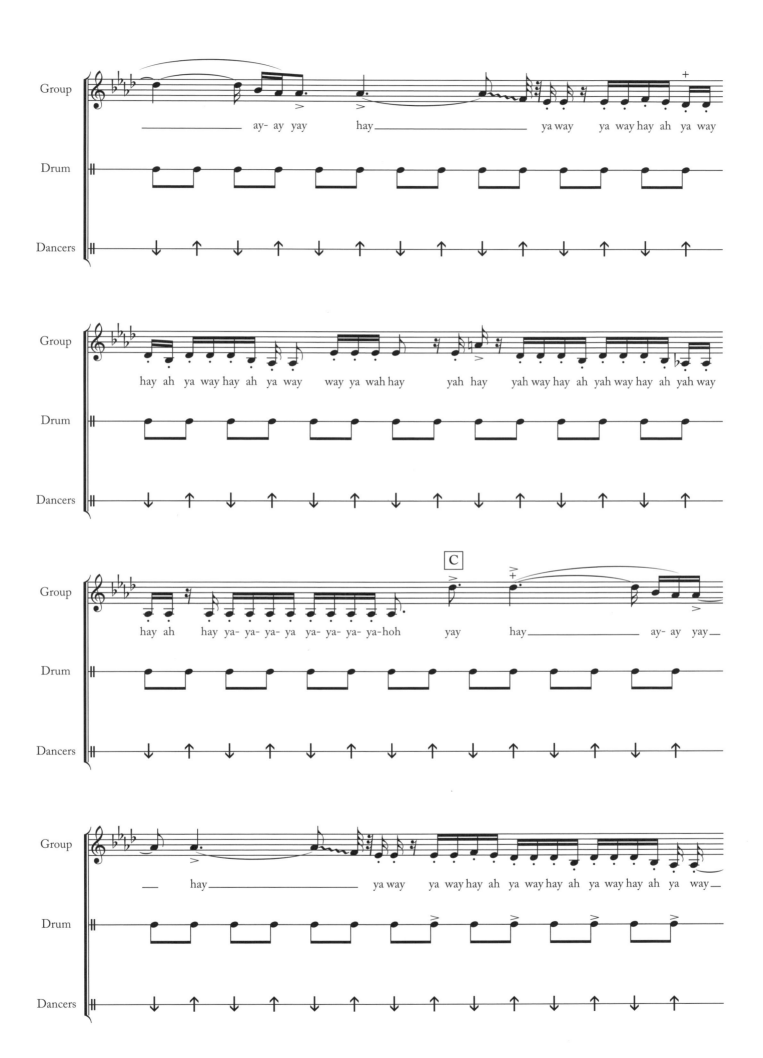

7. Song For All Women's Exhibition

7. Song For All Women's Exhibition

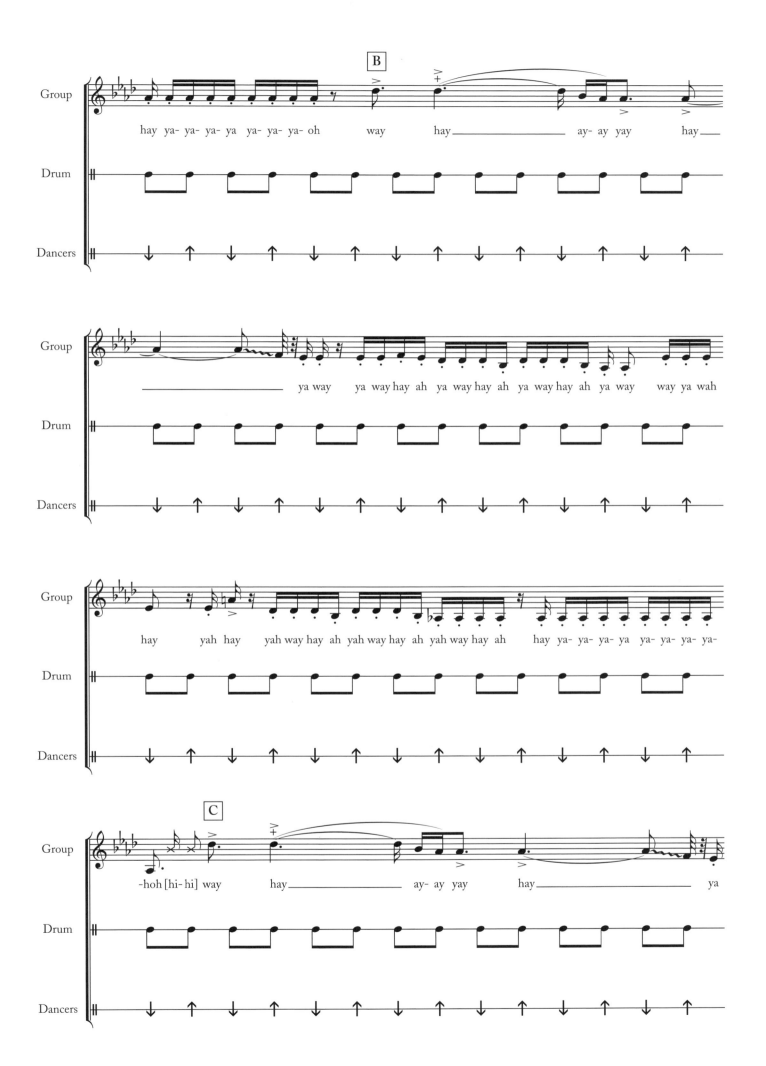

7. Song For All Women's Exhibition

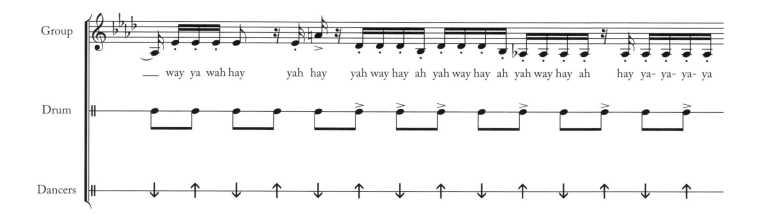
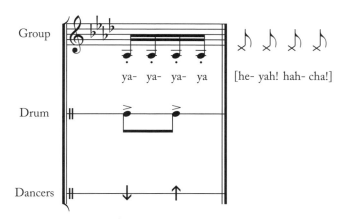

7. Song For All Women's Exhibition

8. TEEN BOYS' SOUTHERN STRAIGHT EXHIBITION

Dottie Tiger's Song

Description. War Dance song, performed by the Cedartree Singers of Falls Church, Virginia. Performers are Michael Rose, John Mark Rose, Jeff Bailey, Erny Zah, Jody Cummings, Vernell Capitan, William A. Sebastian, William Clark, and Echohawk Neconie.

Date. Recorded 5 May 2001 in Los Angeles. Transcribed March 2007.

Bibliographic source. Previously unpublished, transcribed for this collection.

Process. Transcribed by Tara Browner from a recorded performance of the Cedartree Singers.

Form. Length of song is four rounds in A-B-B form, which is standard in the style.

Text. Traditional Southern plains vocables.

Tempos. Energetic but steady, with the exception of short but dramatic increases and decreases in tempo in the transitions between the B and C sections in rounds 3 and 4, which is the norm in the Southern War Dance songs.

Dynamics and accents. Vocal dynamics remain at a level of *forte* throughout. As is standard with Southern Plains songs, dynamic variation is entirely within the drum playing. A single player performs isolated accents, while the group renders larger changes in dynamic level and hard beats in the transitions between the B and C sections.

Tonality. The song begins in F pentatonic (F, G, A, C, D), and modulates up to G pentatonic (G, A, B, E, and D) in round 3.

Variation and ornamentation during performance. None.

Unusual characteristics. None.

8. TEEN BOYS' SOUTHERN STRAIGHT EXHIBITION

Dottie Tiger's Song

Cedartree

8. Teen Boys' Southern Straight Exhibition

8. Teen Boys' Southern Straight Exhibition

8. Teen Boys' Southern Straight Exhibition

9. CONTEST SONG FOR JUNIOR BOYS GRASS AND NORTHERN TRADITIONAL DANCERS

Description. Oglala Lakota Contemporary style word song, made by Jerome LeBeaux, Native Thunder Singers, Pine Ridge Reservation, South Dakota. Performers are Jerome LeBeaux, Aaron Giago, Garfield Steele, Robert Brave Heart, Jenny Ghost Bear, Foster Cournoyer, Virgil Poafpybitty, Tyson Shay, Mike Carlow, and Jermaine Bell.

Date. Recorded 5 May 2001 in Los Angeles. Transcribed April 2007.

Bibliographic source. Previously unpublished, transcribed for this collection.

Process. Transcribed by Tara Browner from a recorded performance of the Native Thunder Singers.

Form. Length of song is four rounds plus a tail (coda) in an unusual form:

A B_1 B_2 B_3 B_4 B_5
      C_1 C_2 C_3 C_4 C_5
(4x)
Tail T_1 T_2 T_3 T_4 T_5

Text. Traditional Northern plains vocables and Lakota text.

Akan makoce ki ota wanna iyokpiya
cante waste yuhopelo
akan makoce ki anpetu
ho wasea ho wasea tawapa
anpetu wastegi ca anpetu
ho wasea ho heni nitawaya

Many people are happy on earth—they are making happy hearts by dancing on earth. This good voice [song] is all of yours on this good day.

Translation by Jerome Lebeaux.

Tempos. Moderate range for this style of song. There is a slight increase in tempo at the beginning of round 3, a common occurrence during live performances.

Dynamics and accents. Vocal dynamics remain at a level of *forte* throughout. As is standard with Northern Plains songs, dynamic variation is entirely within the drum part. A single player performs isolated accents, while the group renders larger changes in dynamic level.

Tonality. D pentatonic (D, E, F♯, A, B) throughout.

Variation and ornamentation during performance. Very little, even in the opening theme statement at the beginning of each round.

Unusual characteristics. The form is unusually complex, while at the same time the melodic variations, even in the opening statement of each round (A), are minimal. Drum accents and location of Honor Beats are standard for a competition song.

9. CONTEST SONG FOR JUNIOR BOYS GRASS AND NORTHERN TRADITIONAL DANCERS

Native Thunder

9. Contest Song for Junior Boys

9. Contest Song for Junior Boys

9. Contest Song for Junior Boys

9. Contest Song for Junior Boys

9. Contest Song for Junior Boys

9. Contest Song for Junior Boys

9. Contest Song for Junior Boys

9. Contest Song for Junior Boys

9. Contest Song for Junior Boys

9. Contest Song for Junior Boys

9. Contest Song for Junior Boys

9. Contest Song for Junior Boys

9. Contest Song for Junior Boys

9. Contest Song for Junior Boys

10. HONOR SONG FOR BEN WOLF'S FAMILY

Description. Honor Song in a War Dance style, performed by the Cedartree Singers of Falls Church, Virginia. Performers are Michael Rose, John Mark Rose, Jeff Bailey, Erny Zah, Jody Cummings, Vernell Capitan, William A. Sebastian, William Clark, and Echohawk Neconie.

Date. Recorded 5 May 2001 in Los Angeles. Transcribed September 2005.

Bibliographic source. Previously unpublished, transcribed for this collection.

Process. Transcribed by Tara Browner from a recorded performance of the Cedartree Singers.

Form. Length of song is eleven rounds plus a tail (coda) in an A-B-B form, which is standard in the style.

Text. Traditional Southern plains vocables.

Tempos. Moderate range and steady. There are short but dramatic increases and decreases in tempo in the transitions between the B and C sections in rounds 6, 8, and 11, which is the norm in the Southern War Dance songs tradition.

Dynamics and accents. Vocal dynamics remain at a level of *forte* throughout. As is standard with Southern Plains songs, dynamic variation is entirely within the drum playing. A single player performs isolated accents, while the group renders larger changes in dynamic level and hard beats in the transitions between the B and C sections.

Tonality. The song begins in a mixture of F major and minor pentatonic (F, G, A♭, B♭, C, D, and E♭), alternating modes between phrases (minor in the A sections, major in the B and C sections). In round 5 it modulates up to a mixed G major and minor pentatonic (G, A, B♭, C, E, F and D), and alternating modes in the same pattern.

Variation and ornamentation during performance. Rounds 5, 6, 8, and 11 feature truncated opening statements of the theme by the head singer. This is common in later rounds in the Southern style, and ties in with the increase in tempo.

Unusual characteristics. The use of both major and minor pentatonic modes within the same song is unusual, but the pattern of opening in minor and changing to major mode can found in some War Dance songs from Central Oklahoma (Ponca and Pawnee).

10. HONOR SONG FOR BEN WOLF'S FAMILY

Cedartree

10. Honor Song for Ben Wolf's Family

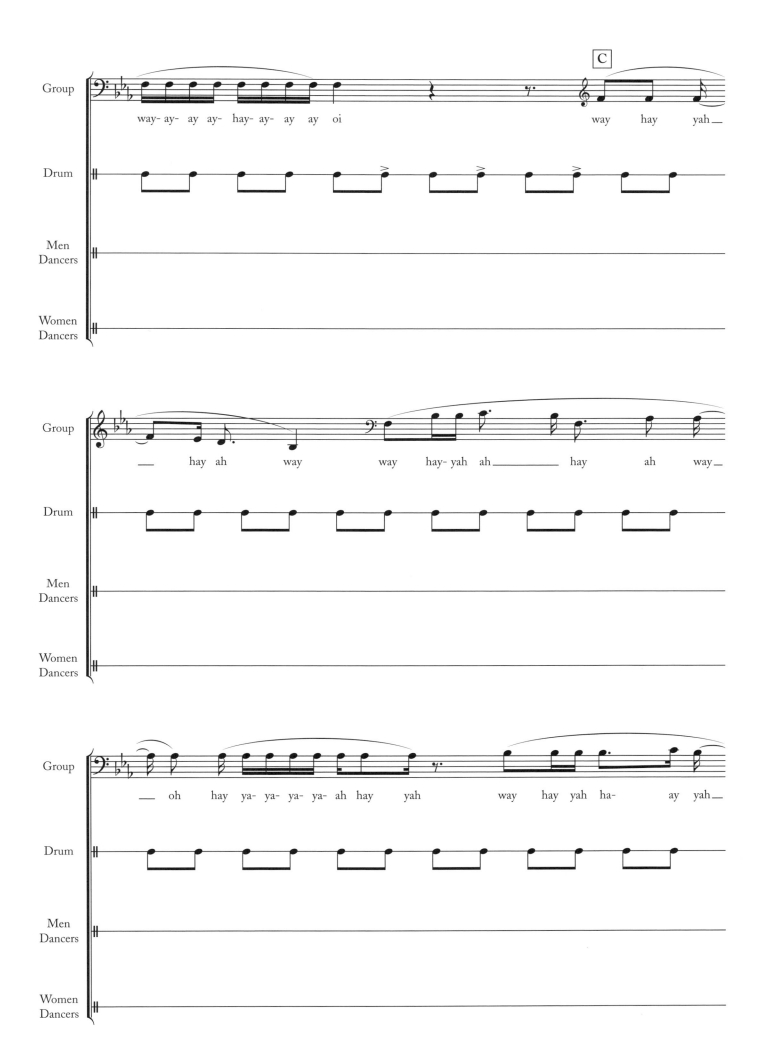

10. Honor Song for Ben Wolf's Family

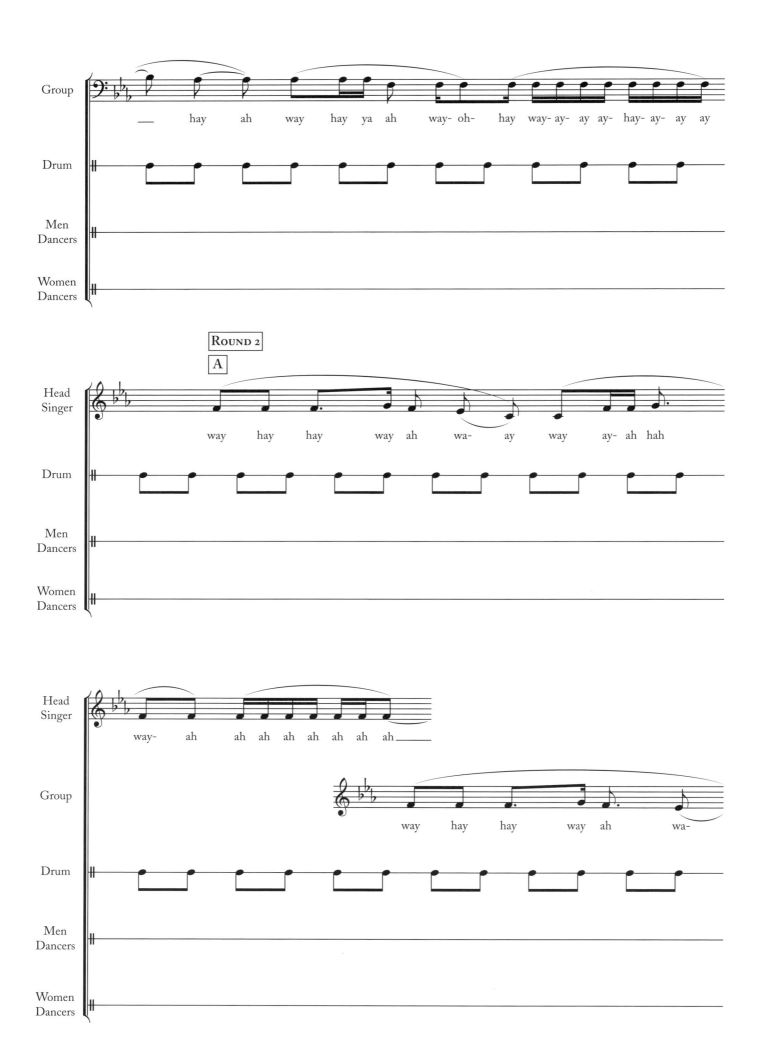

10. Honor Song for Ben Wolf's Family

10. Honor Song for Ben Wolf's Family

10. Honor Song for Ben Wolf's Family

10. Honor Song for Ben Wolf's Family

122   10. Honor Song for Ben Wolf's Family

10. Honor Song for Ben Wolf's Family

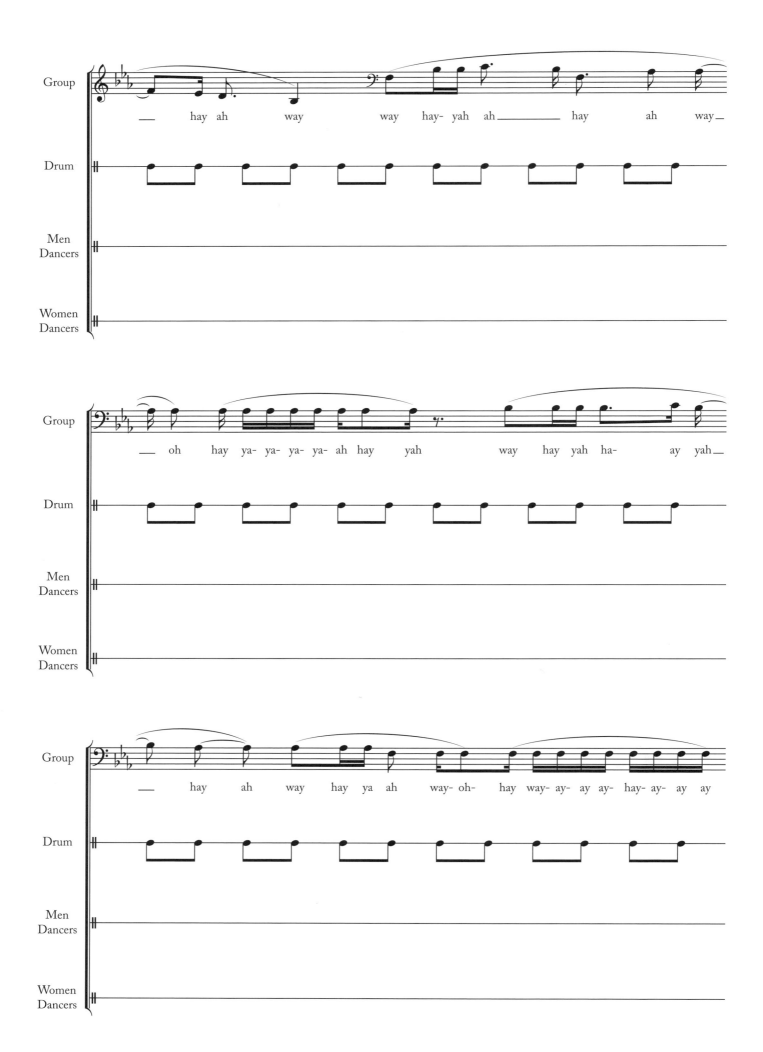

10. Honor Song for Ben Wolf's Family

10. Honor Song for Ben Wolf's Family

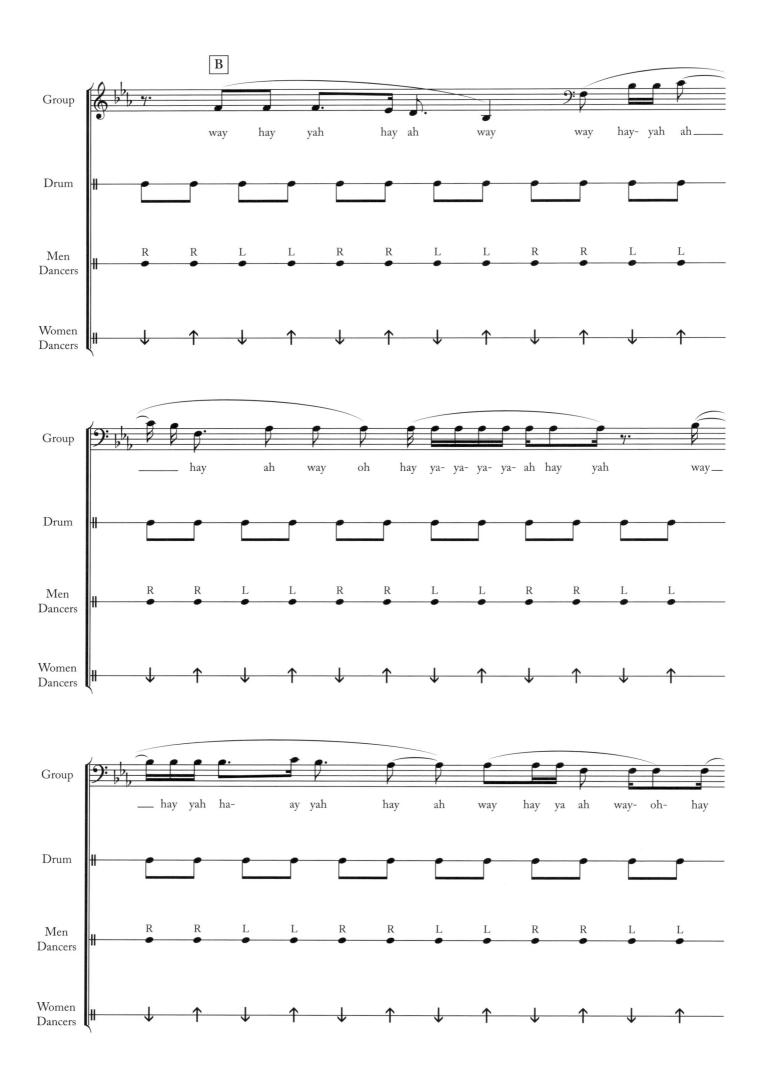

10. Honor Song for Ben Wolf's Family

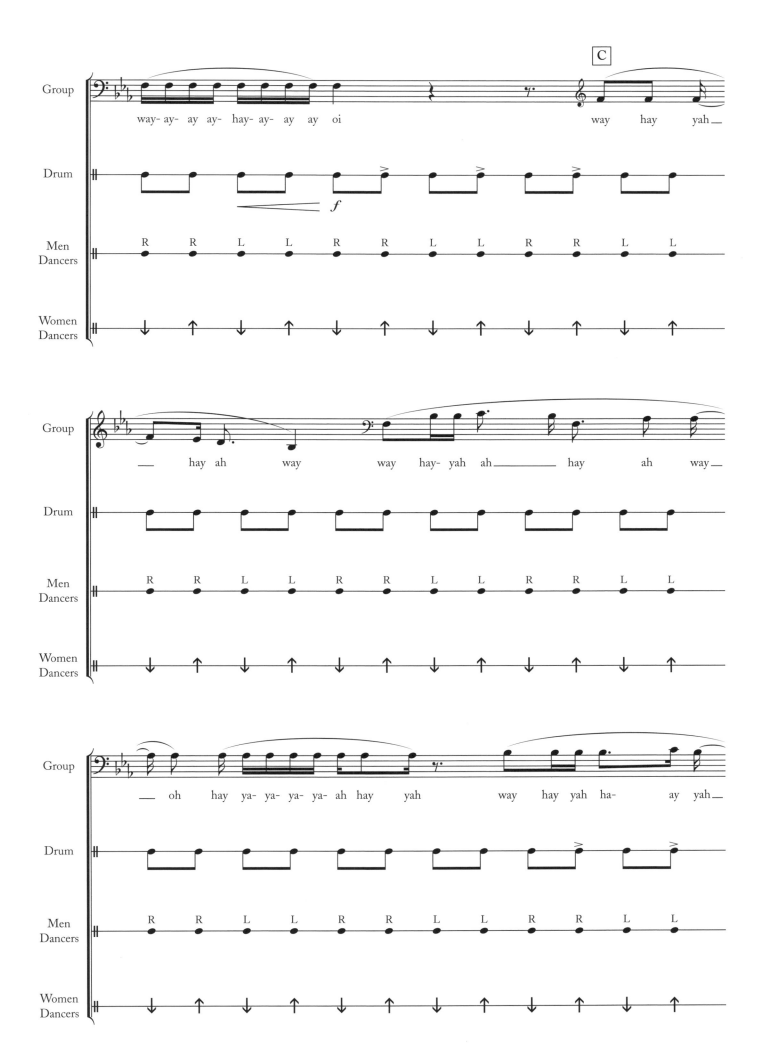

10. Honor Song for Ben Wolf's Family

10. Honor Song for Ben Wolf's Family

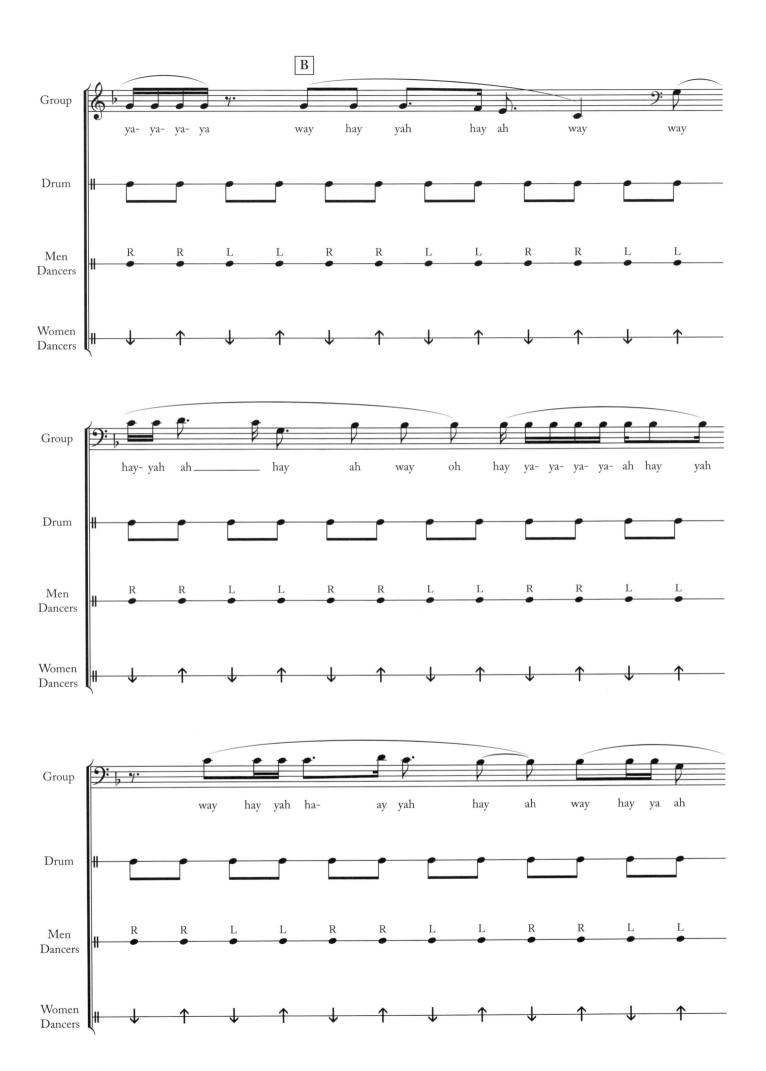

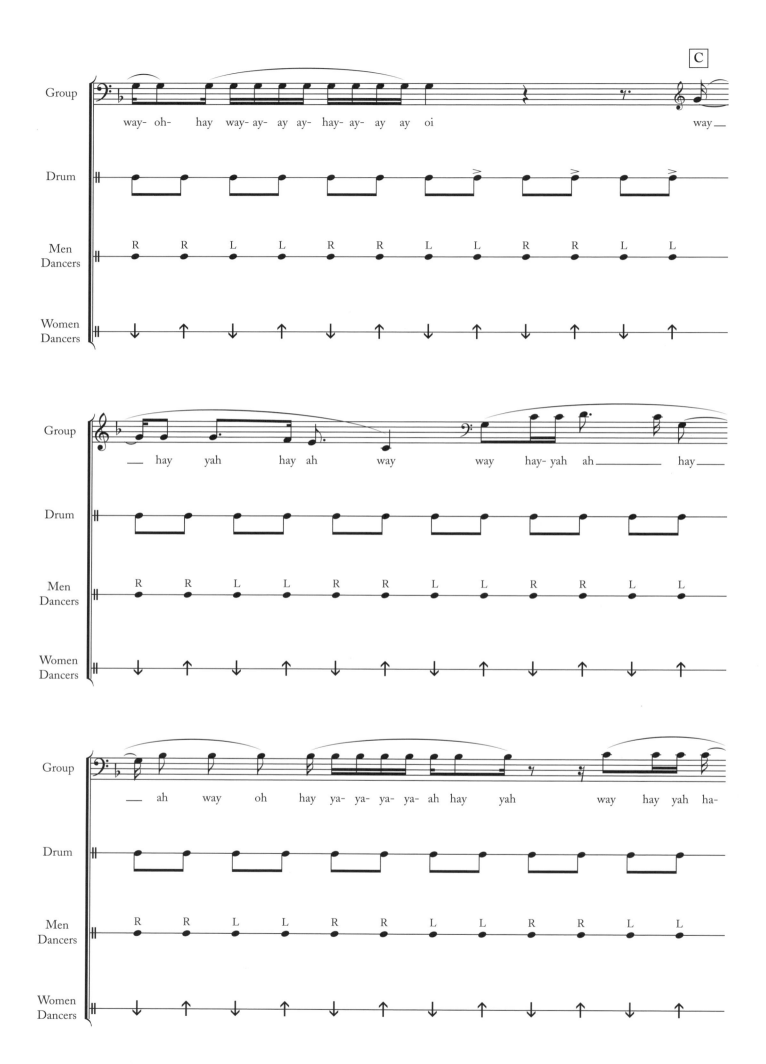

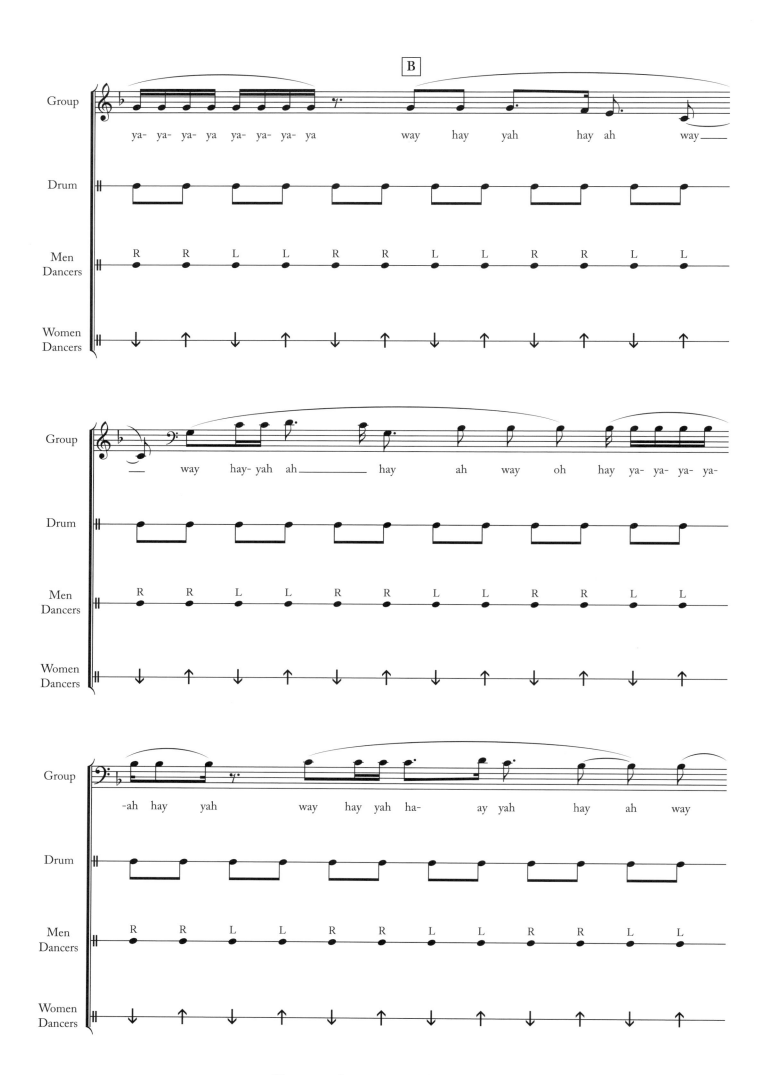

10. Honor Song for Ben Wolf's Family

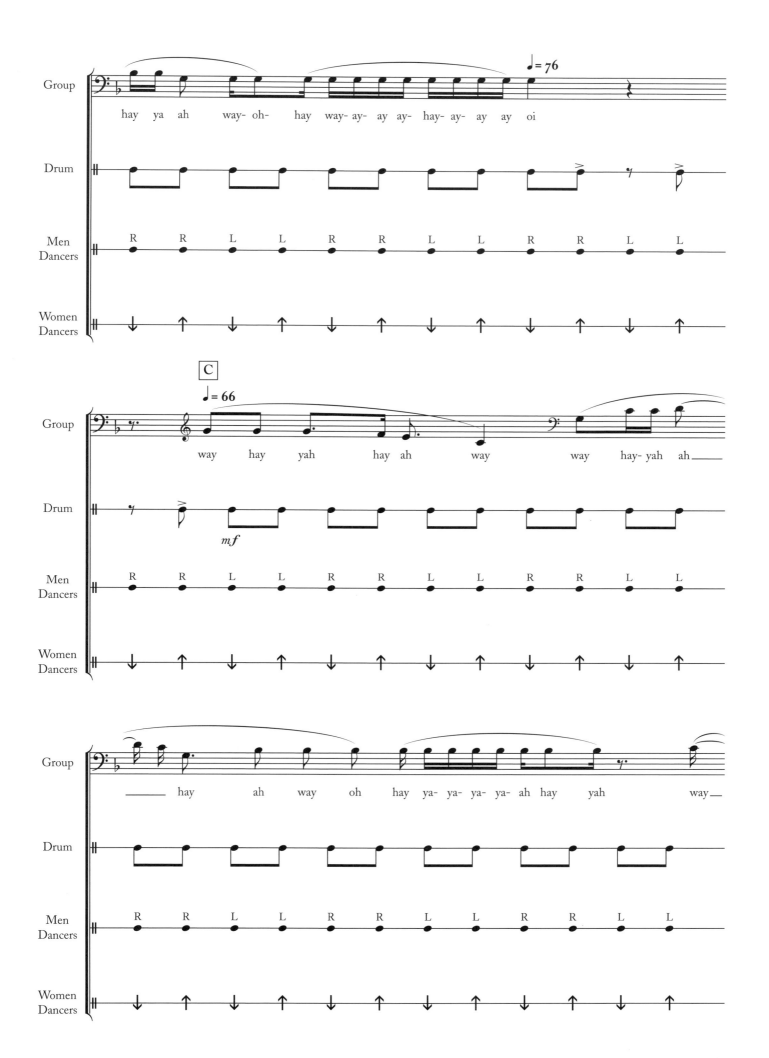

10. Honor Song for Ben Wolf's Family

10. Honor Song for Ben Wolf's Family

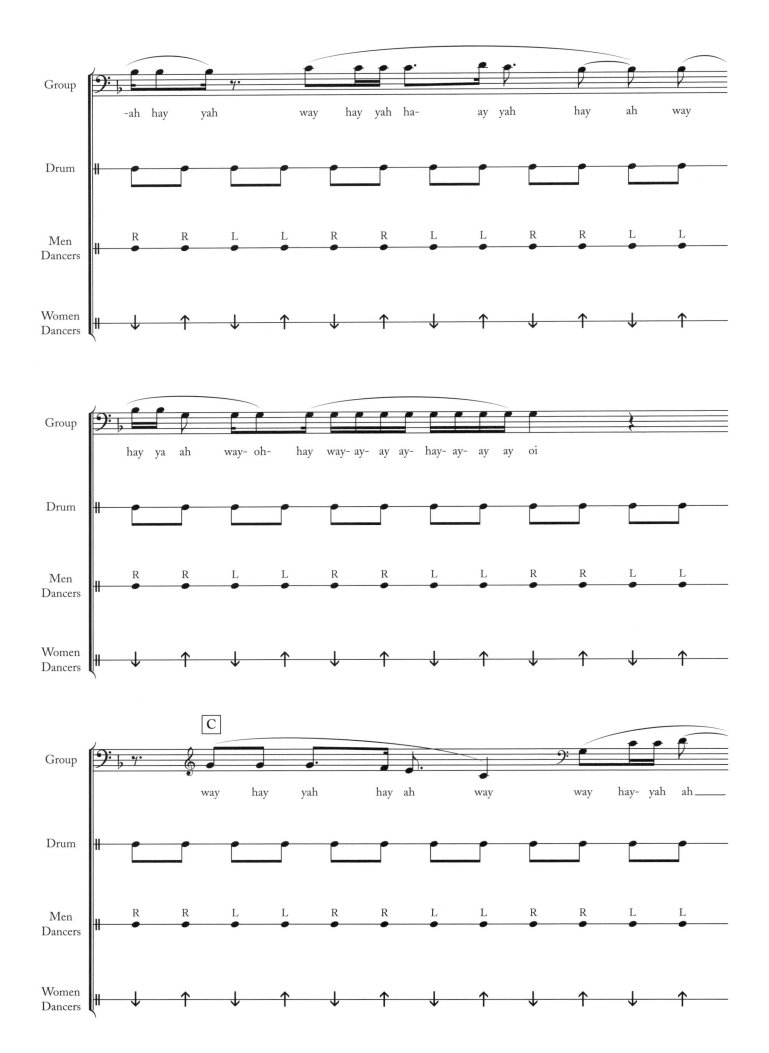

10. Honor Song for Ben Wolf's Family

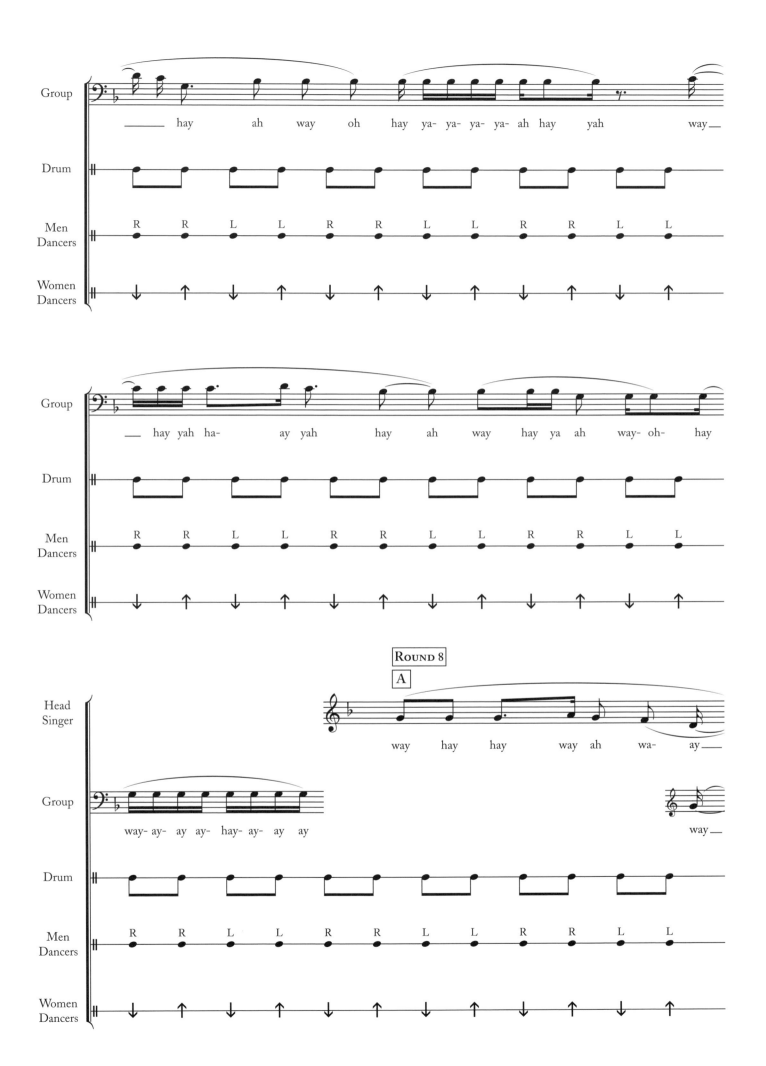

10. Honor Song for Ben Wolf's Family

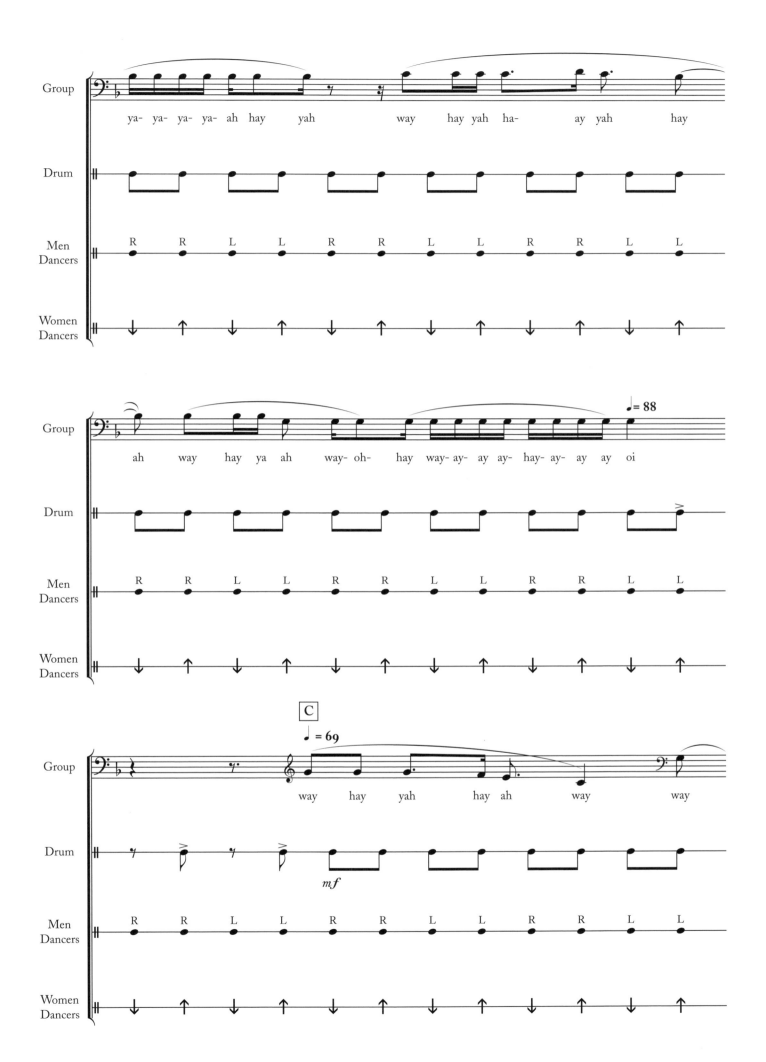

10. Honor Song for Ben Wolf's Family

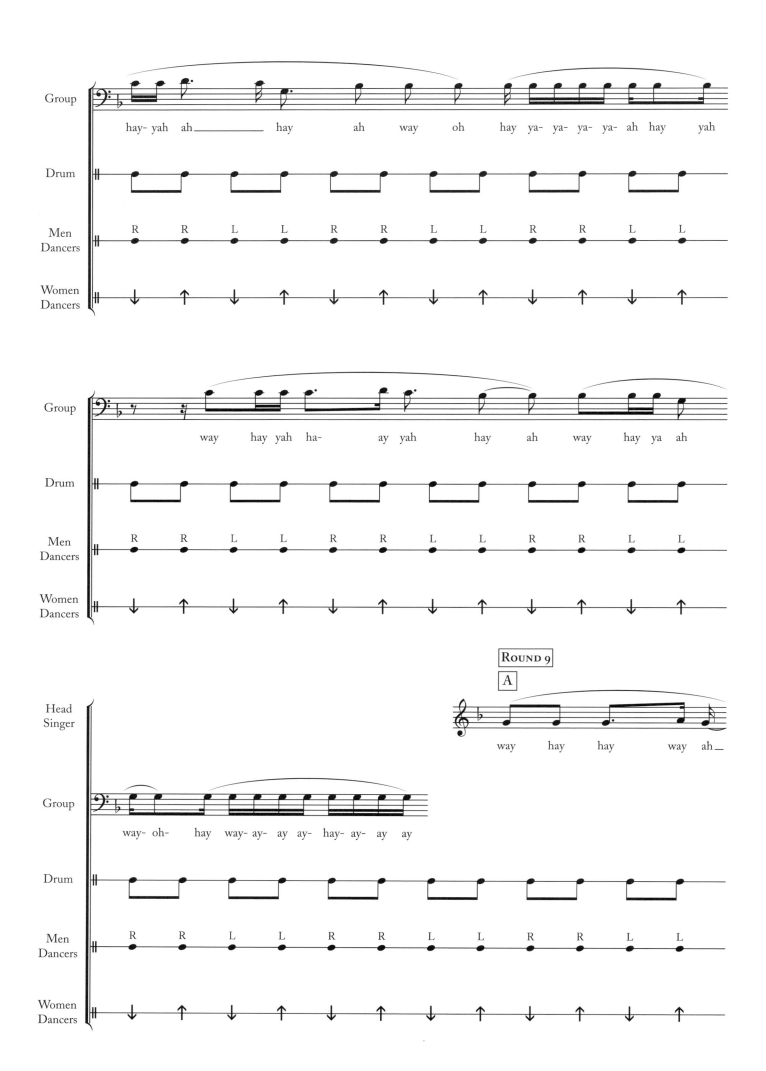

10. Honor Song for Ben Wolf's Family

10. Honor Song for Ben Wolf's Family

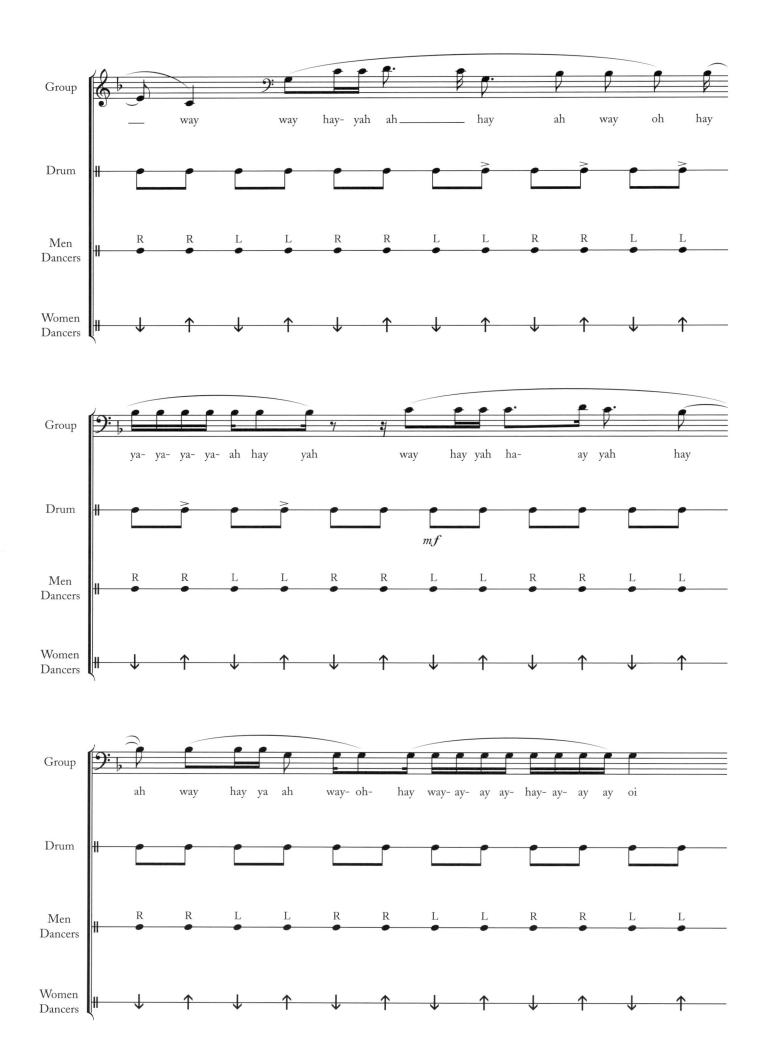

10. Honor Song for Ben Wolf's Family

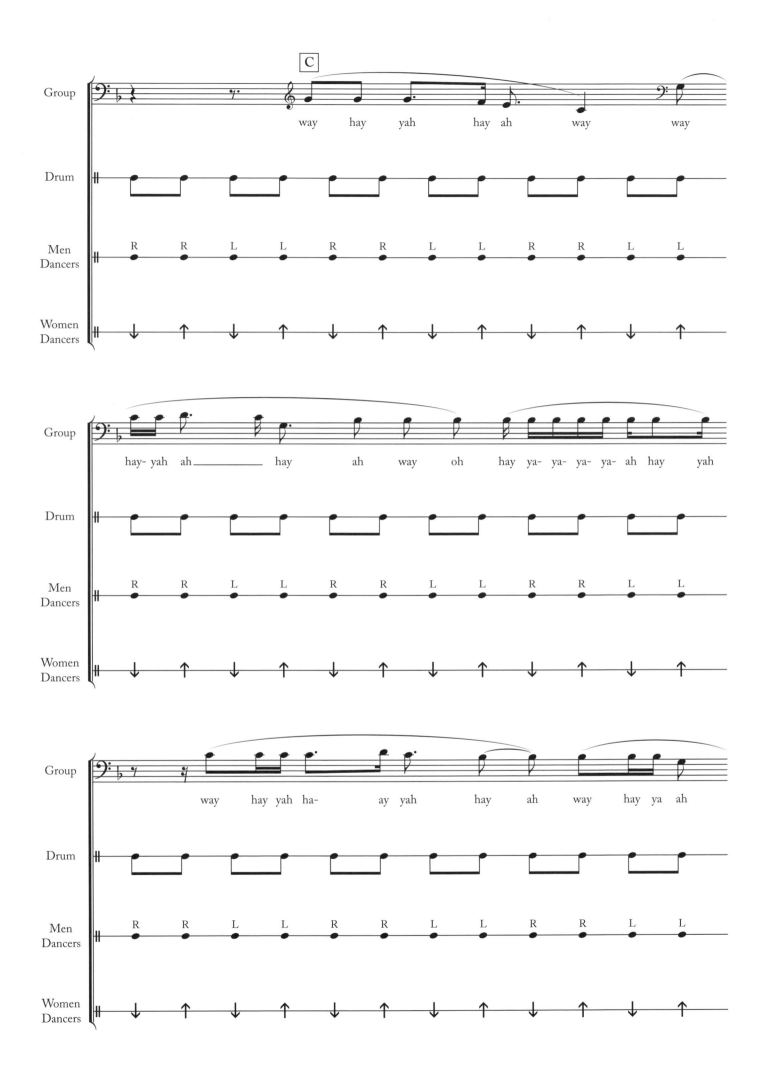

10. Honor Song for Ben Wolf's Family

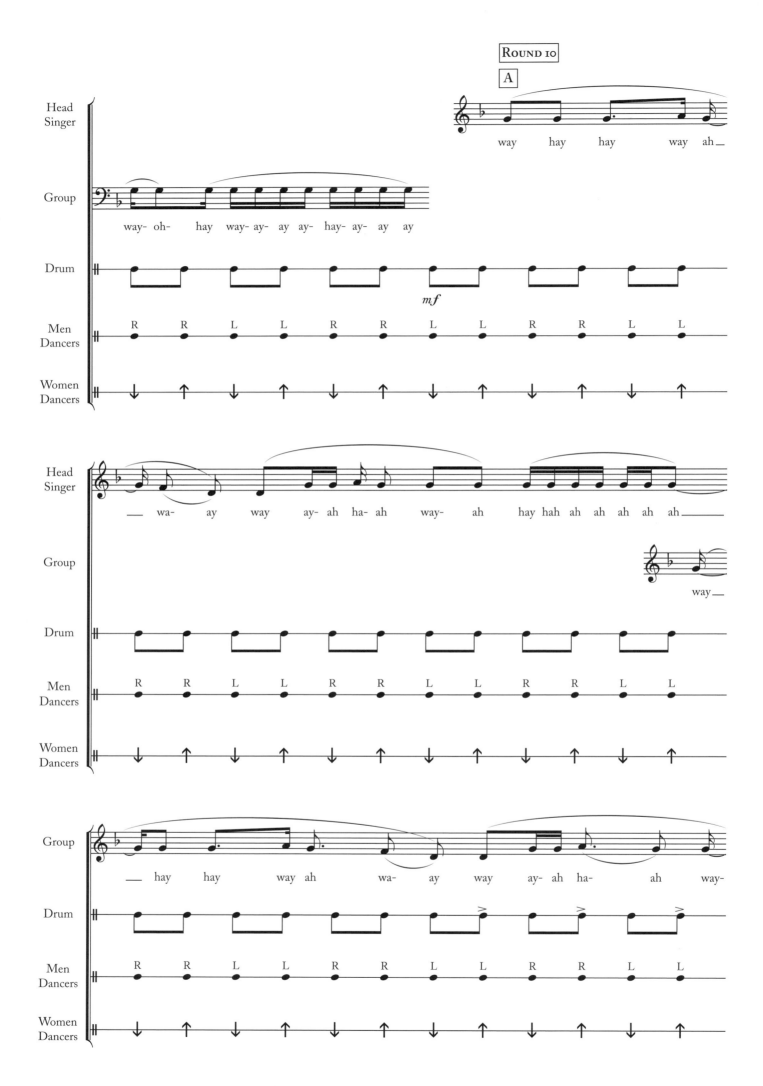

10. Honor Song for Ben Wolf's Family

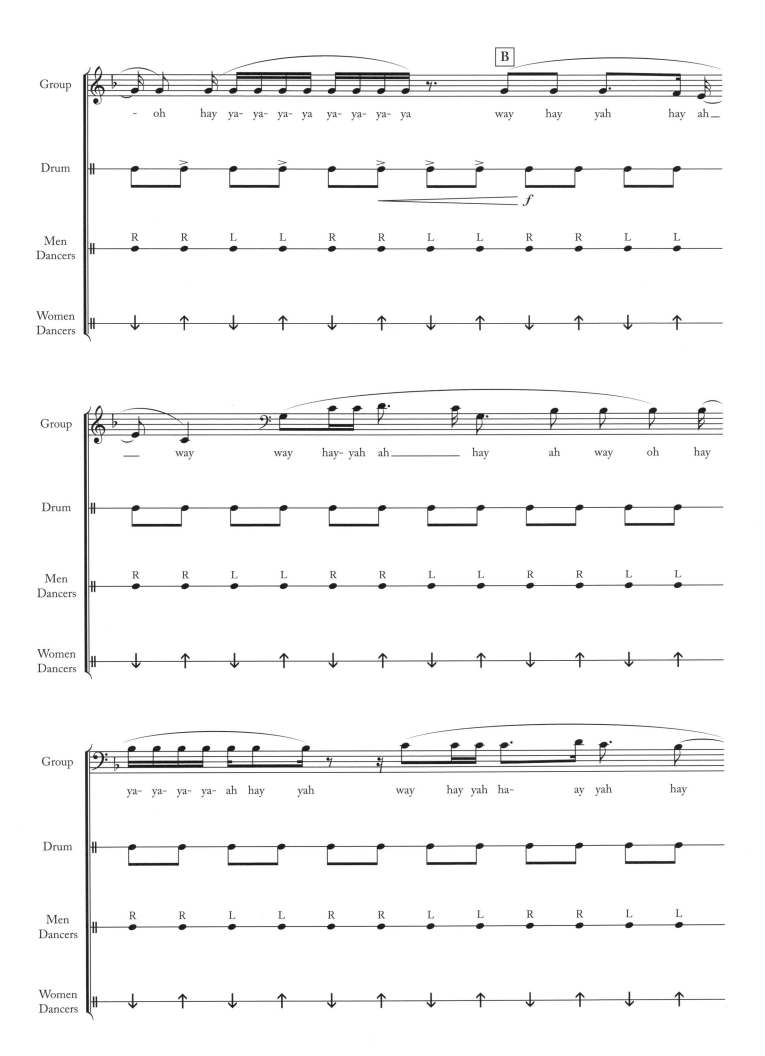

10. Honor Song for Ben Wolf's Family

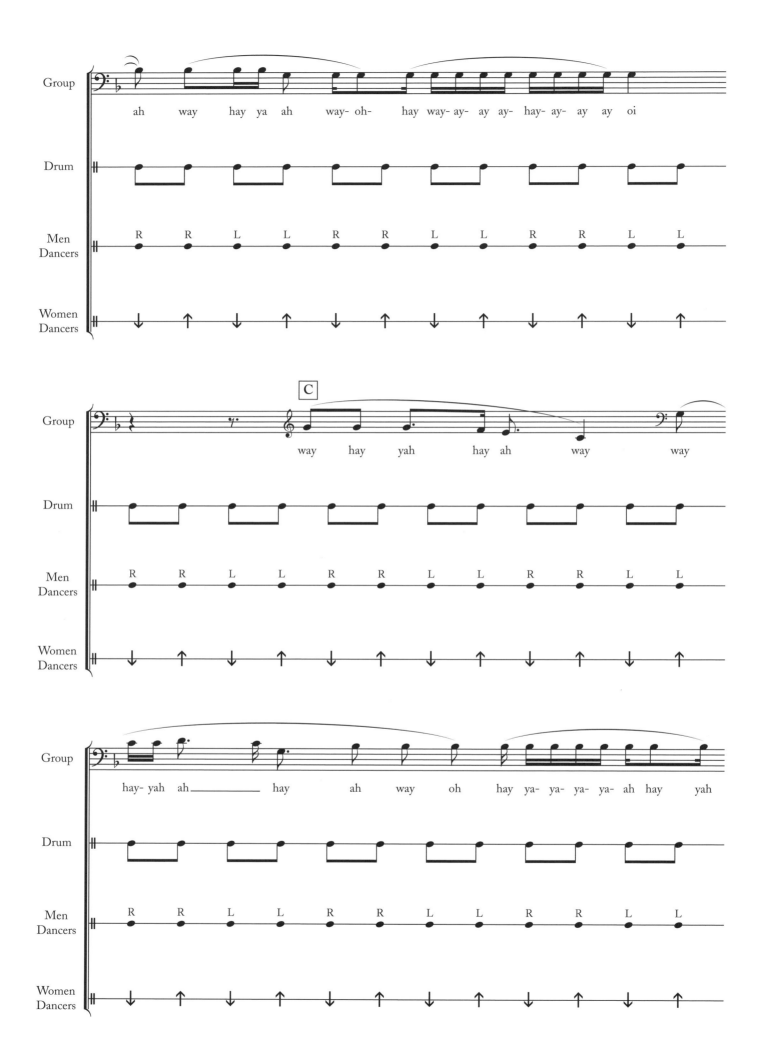

10. Honor Song for Ben Wolf's Family

10. Honor Song for Ben Wolf's Family

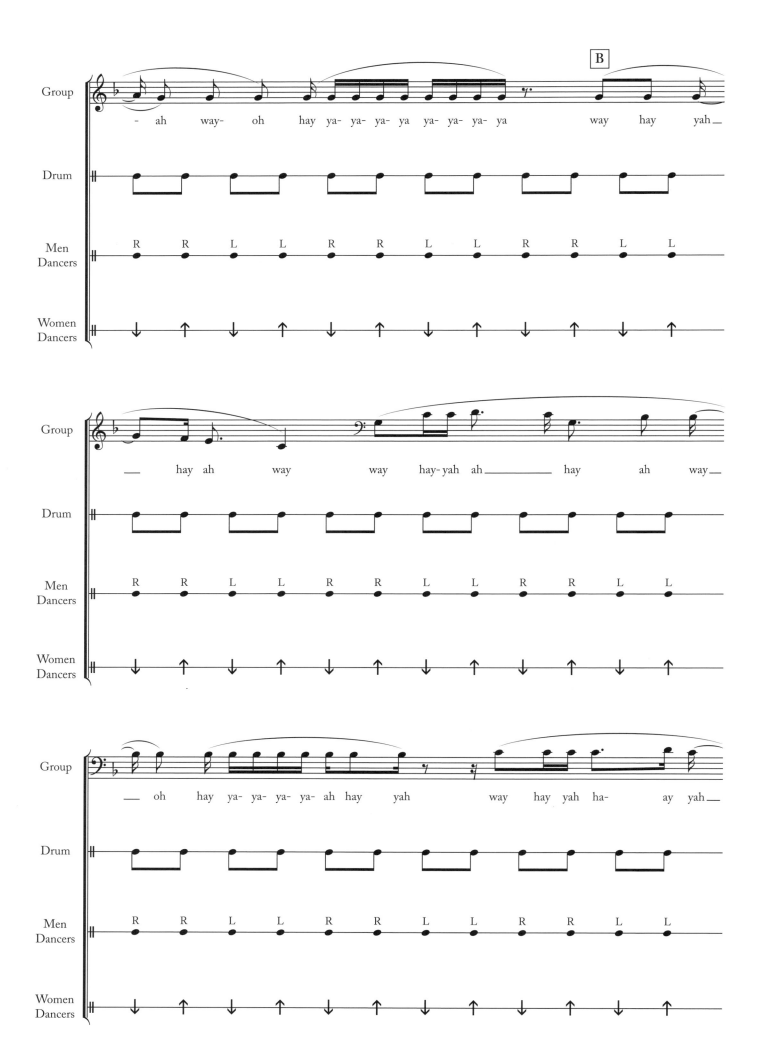

10. Honor Song for Ben Wolf's Family

10. Honor Song for Ben Wolf's Family

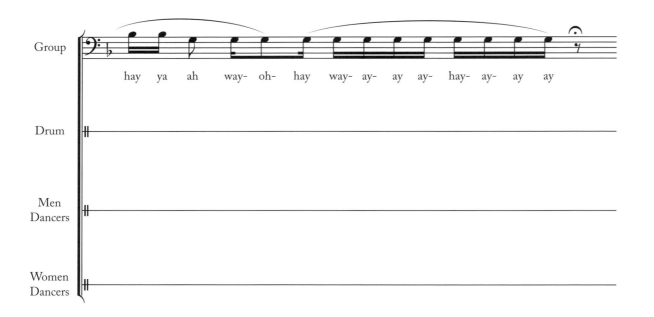
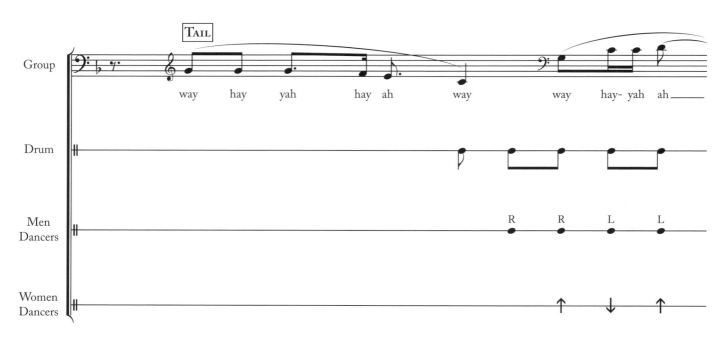

10. Honor Song for Ben Wolf's Family

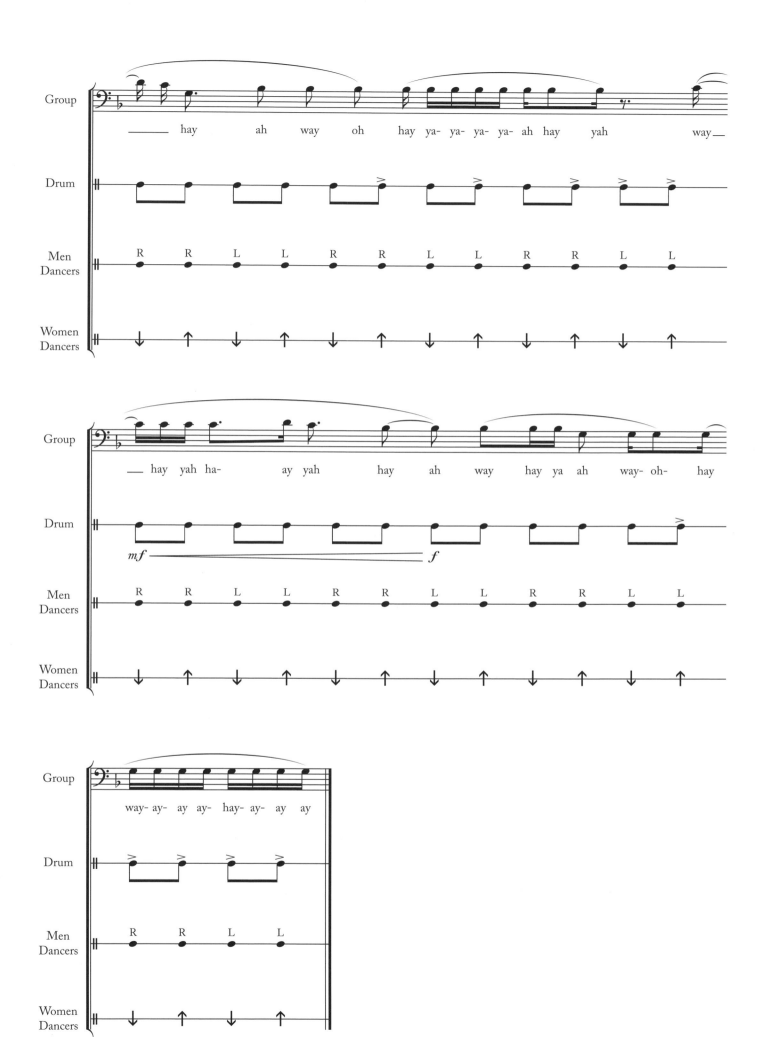

10. Honor Song for Ben Wolf's Family

11. STRAIGHT INTERTRIBAL SONG

Description. Oglala Lakota Contemporary straight song, Native Thunder Singers, Pine Ridge Reservation, South Dakota. Performers are Jerome LeBeaux, Aaron Giago, Garfield Steele, Robert Brave Heart, Jenny Ghost Bear, Foster Cournoyer, Virgil Poafpybitty, Tyson Shay, Mike Carlow, and Jermaine Bell.

Date. Recorded 5 May 2001 in Los Angeles. Transcribed September 2001.

Bibliographic source. Previously unpublished, transcribed for this collection.

Process. Transcribed by Tara Browner from a recorded performance of the Native Thunder Singers.

Form. Length of song is six rounds plus a tail (coda) in an A-B1-B2—C1-C2 form, which is fairly standard in the style, although rarer than A-B-B.

Text. Traditional Northern plains vocables.

Tempos. Moderate range for this style of song. There is a gradual increase in tempo throughout the song, a common occurrence during live performances.

Dynamics and accents. Vocal dynamics remain at a level of *forte* throughout. As is usual with Northern Plains songs, dynamic variation is entirely within the drum part. A single player performs isolated accents, while the group renders larger changes in dynamic level.

Tonality. The song begins in F-sharp pentatonic (F♯, G♯, A♯, C♯, D♯), modulates up to G pentatonic (G, A, B, E, and D) in round 4, and A-flat pentatonic (A♭, B♭, C, E♭, F) in round 6 through the end of the tail.

Variation and ornamentation during performance. Melodic variations are found in the solo opening statement of each round, and in the sixteenth-note pattern at the end of the first long phrase after B. There are also rhythmic variations in the unpitched vocal exclamations during in the first ending. Ornamentation occurs in the form of lower-octave grace notes leading into longer sustained notes.

Unusual characteristics. This song progressively modulates up a full tone (by half steps), a common musical intensification practice in Southern songs, but rare in Northern live performance. The rule in Northern singing is for songs gradually to drop in pitch as singers are often unable to sustain the pitch level established during the song's opening statement, usually sung by the group's best singer. Also, the short rhythmic/melodic interjection ("hay yah ho") from the primary theme located seven and a half beats after letter B1 (and C1) is exceptional.

11. STRAIGHT INTERTRIBAL SONG

Native Thunder

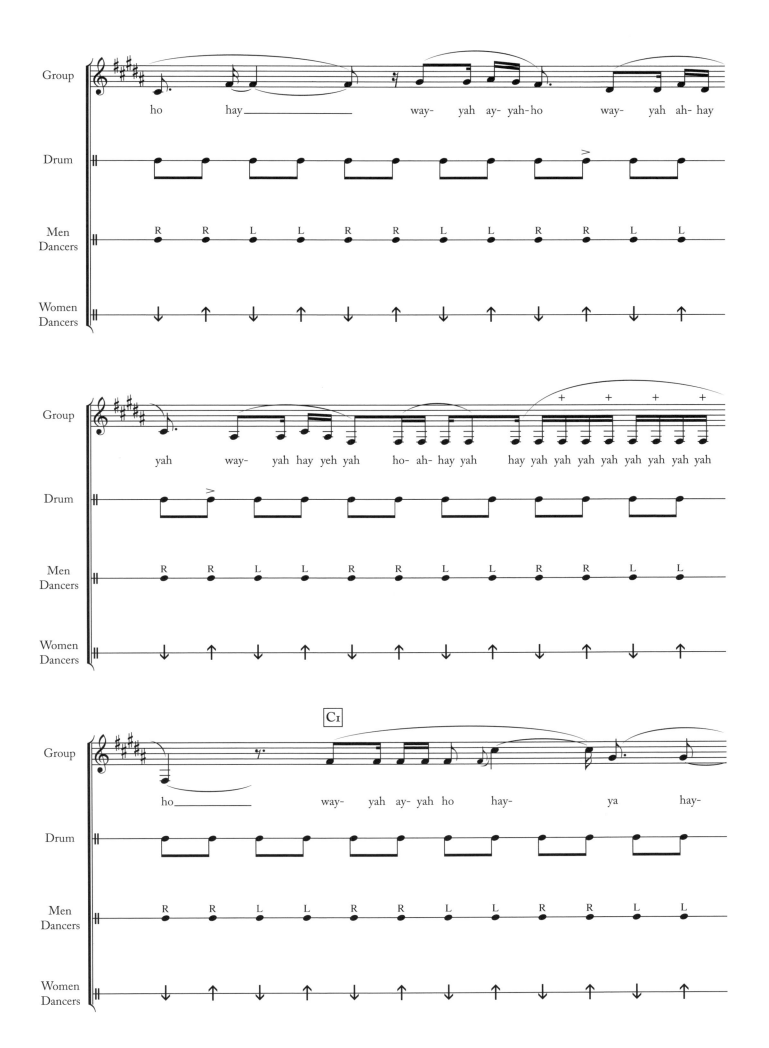

11. Straight Intertribal Song

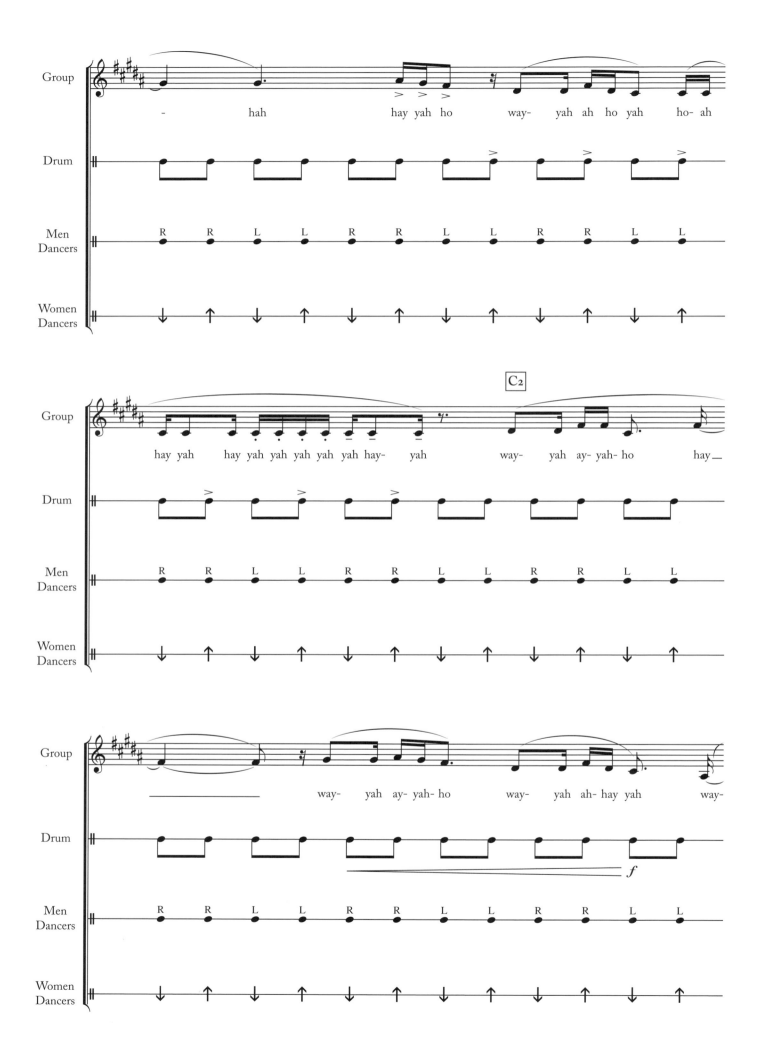

11. Straight Intertribal Song

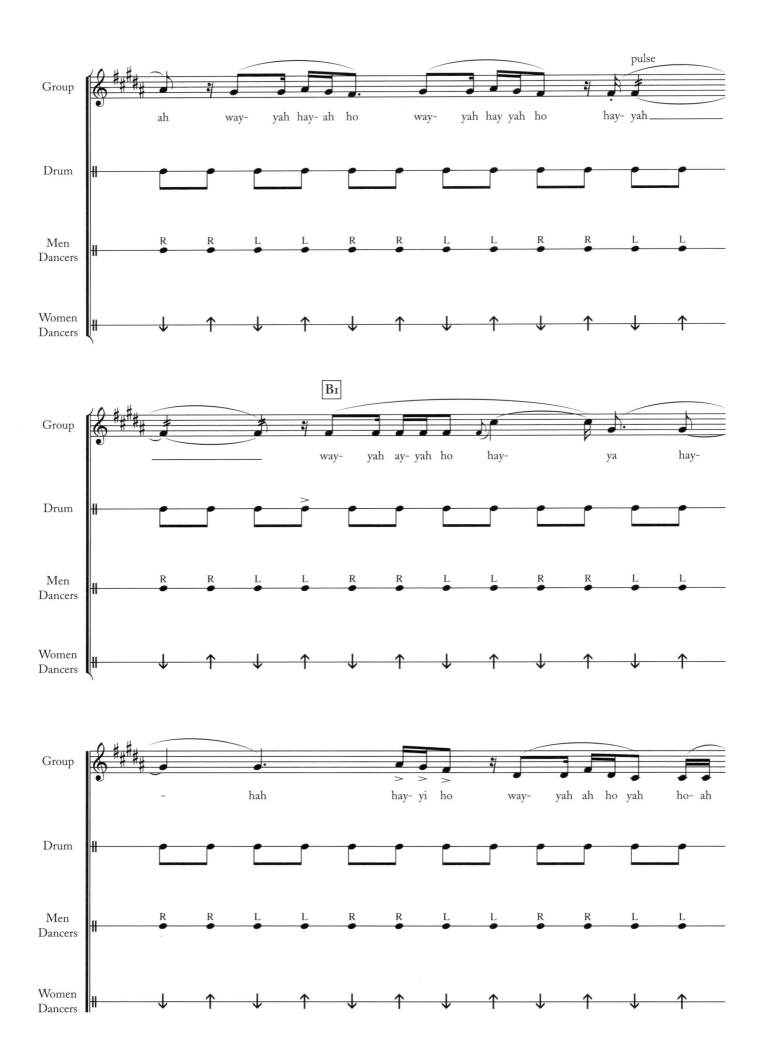

11. Straight Intertribal Song

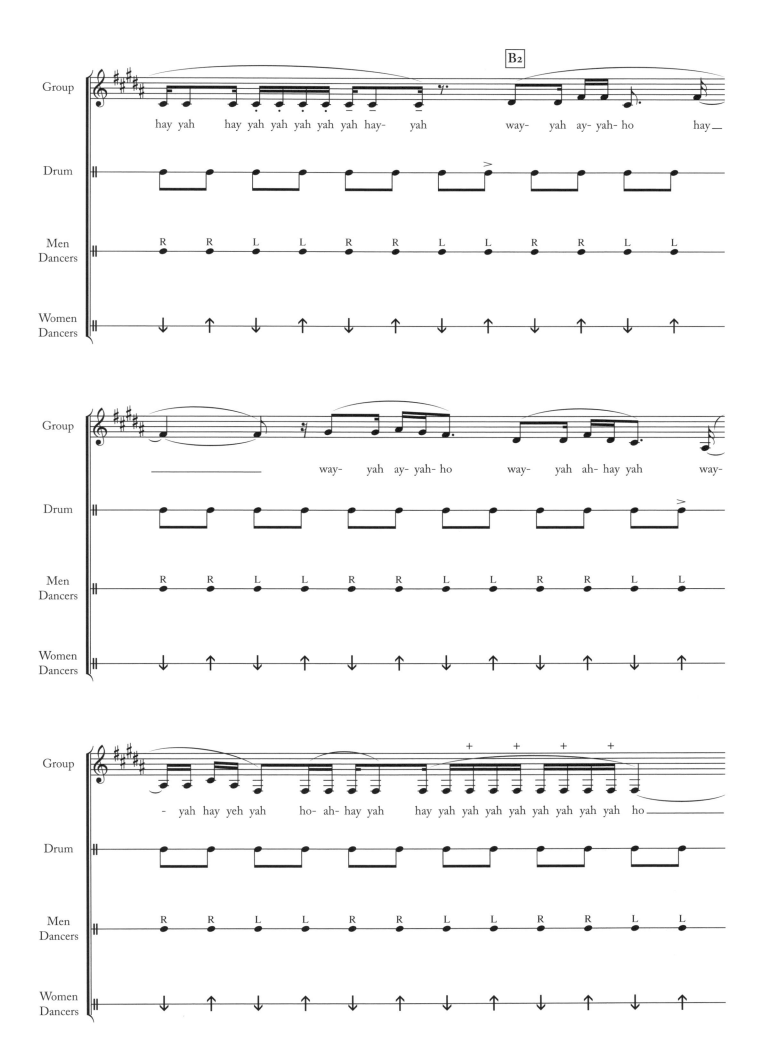

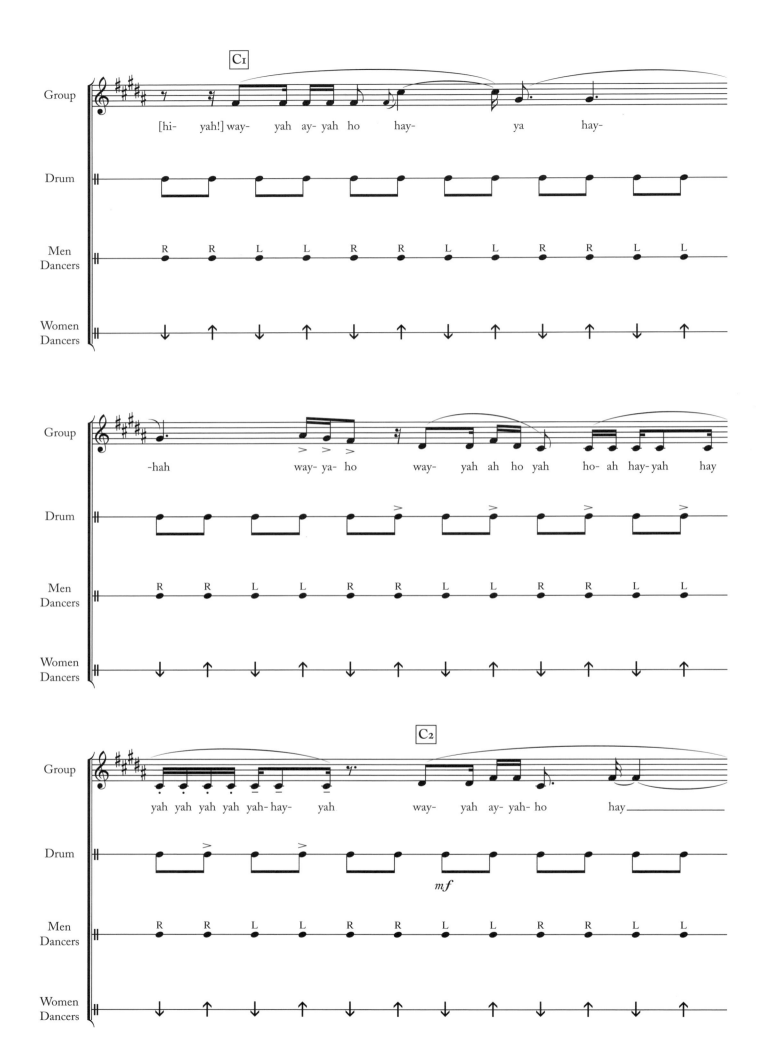

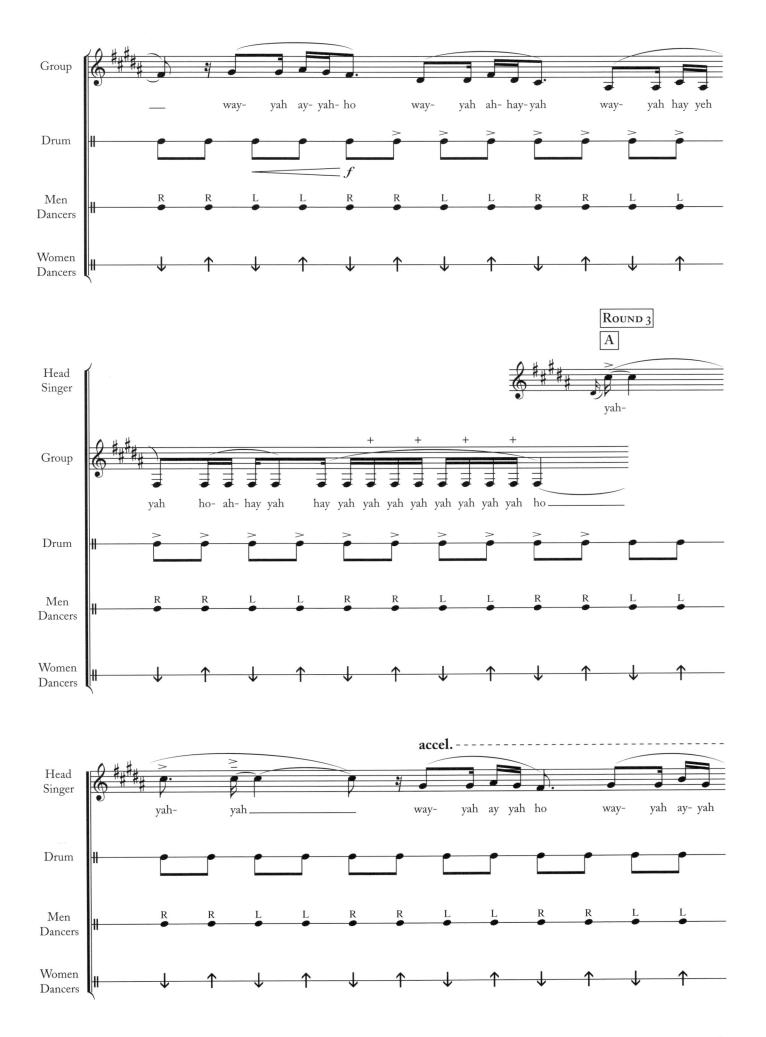

11. Straight Intertribal Song

11. Straight Intertribal Song

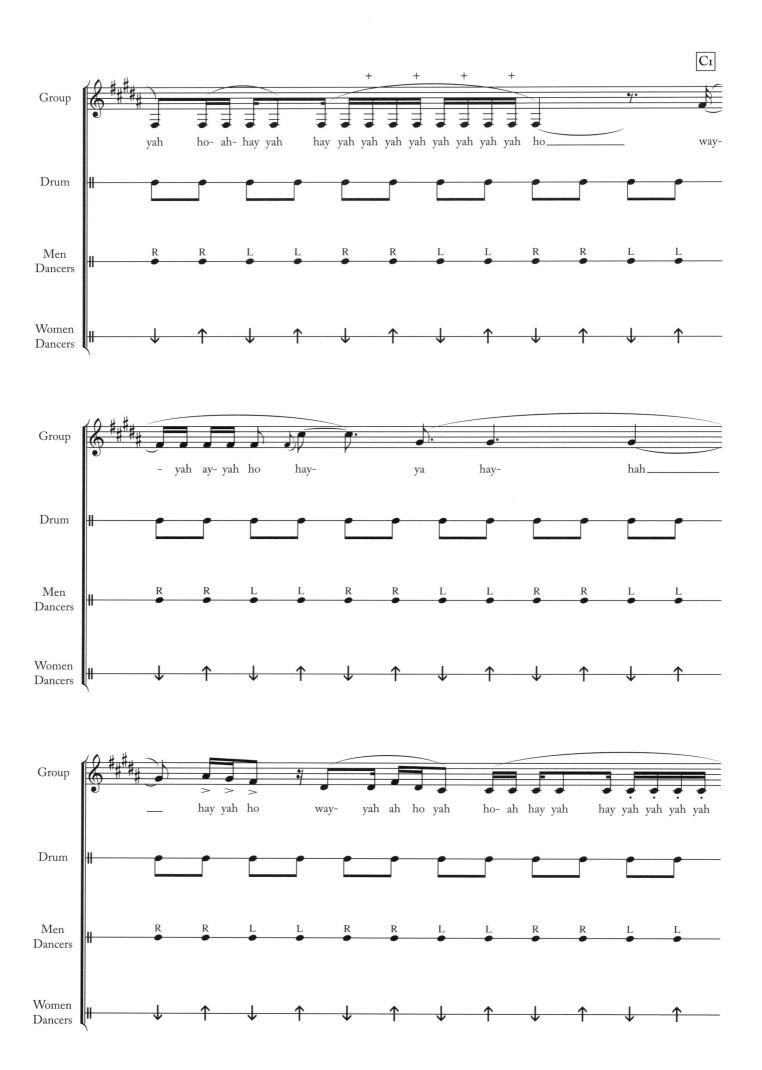

11. Straight Intertribal Song

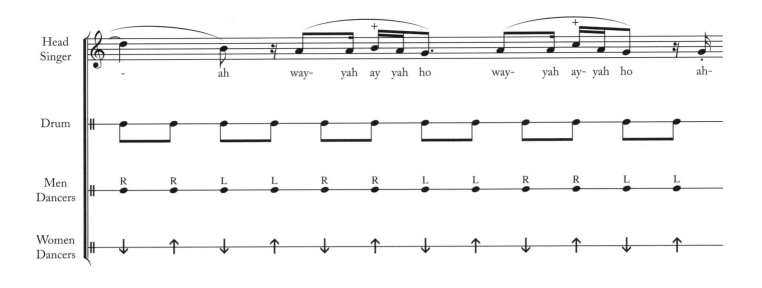
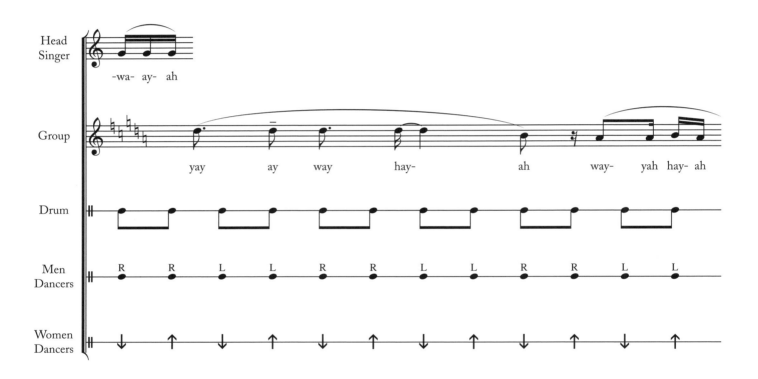

11. Straight Intertribal Song

11. Straight Intertribal Song

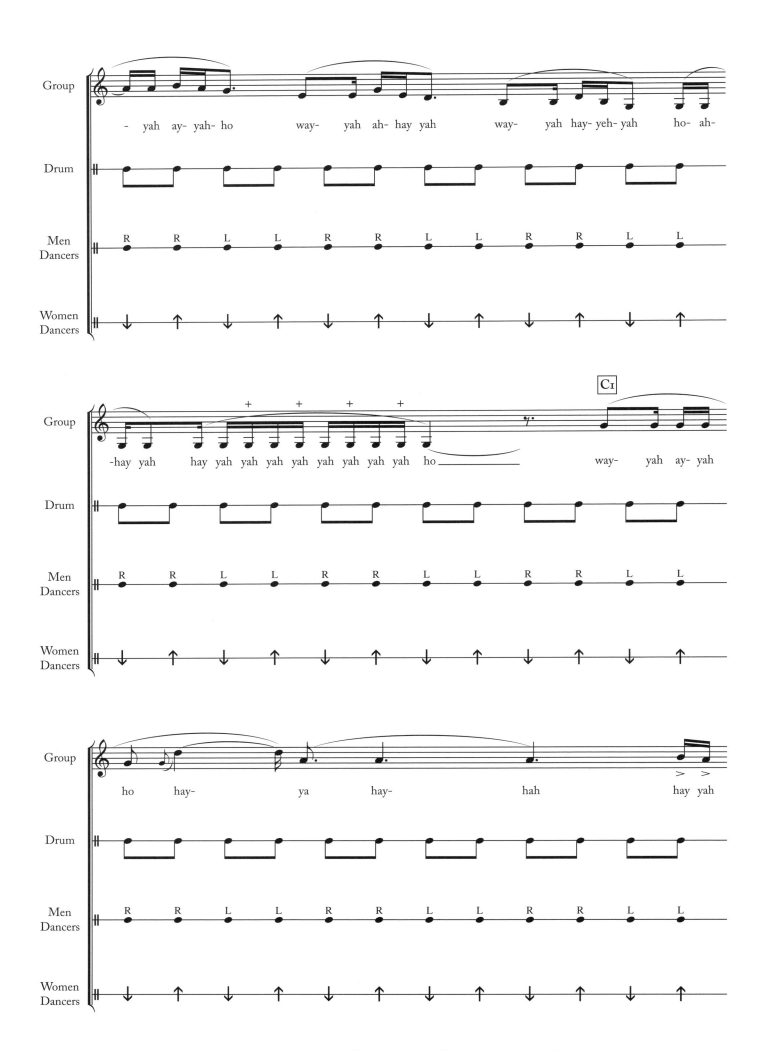

11. Straight Intertribal Song

11. Straight Intertribal Song

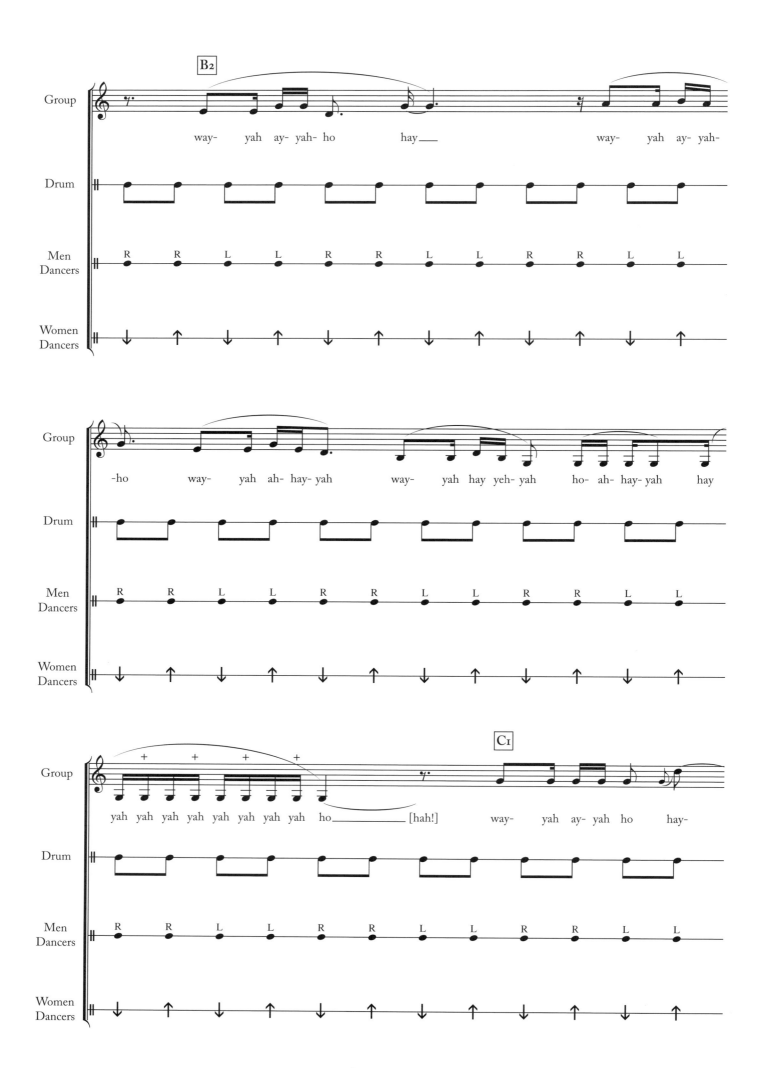

11. Straight Intertribal Song

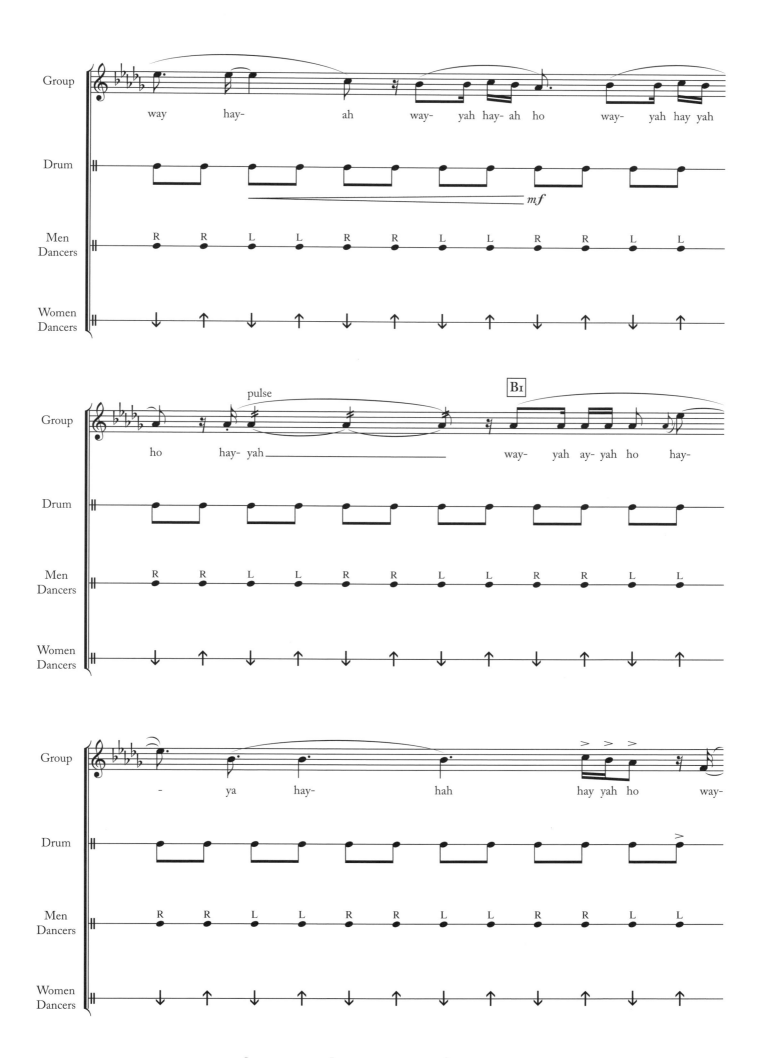

11. Straight Intertribal Song

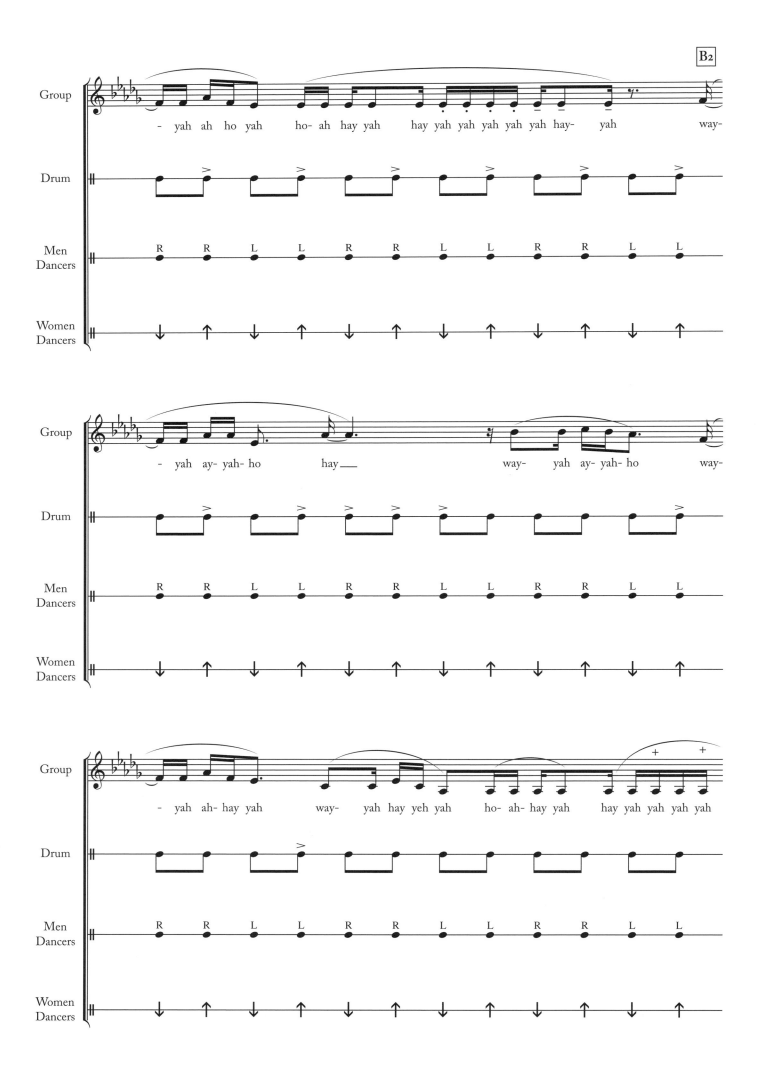

11. Straight Intertribal Song

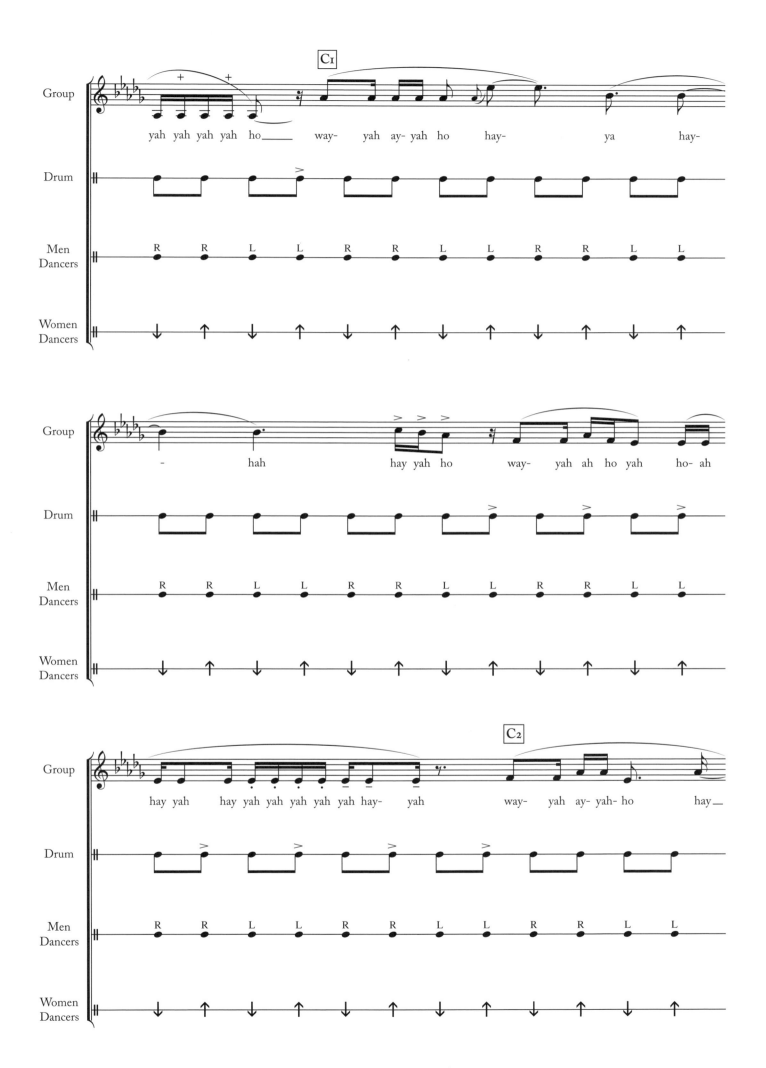

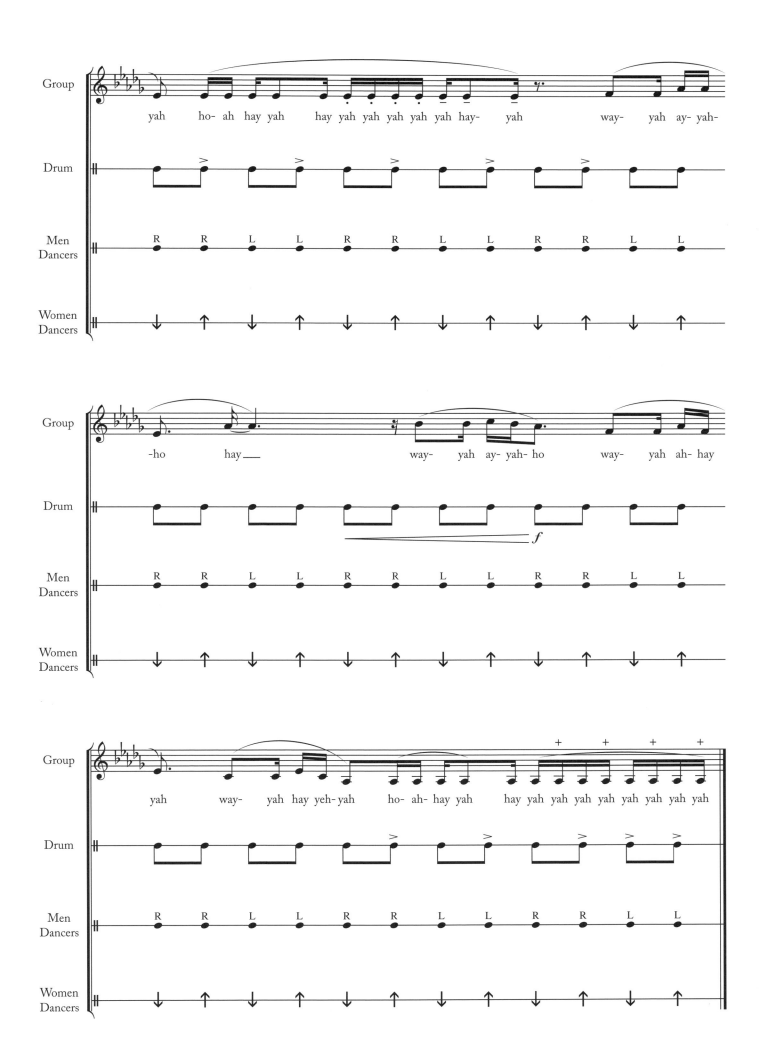
11. Straight Intertribal Song

12. FLAG SONG

Wapaha Olowan

Description. Lakota Flag song, traditional, performed by the Native Thunder Singers, Pine Ridge Reservation, South Dakota. Performers are Jerome LeBeaux, Aaron Giago, Garfield Steele, Robert Brave Heart, Jenny Ghost Bear, Foster Cournoyer, Virgil Poafpybitty, Tyson Shay, Mike Carlow, and Jermaine Bell. This Flag Song is a standard part of every Lakota Drum Group's repertory, and is usually performed before the retreat at the end of a pow-wow session. It is one of at least six known Lakota/Sioux Flag Songs, but because it has no words is not considered a National Anthem.

Date. Recorded 5 May 2001 in Los Angeles. Transcribed March 2007.

Bibliographic source. Previously unpublished, transcribed for this collection.

Process. Transcribed by Tara Browner from a recorded performance of the Native Thunder Singers.

Form. Two rounds, A-B form, with opening incipit and then two repeats by the group of the melodic motif. At the end of round 2, the drum drops out and singers only finish the song.

Text. Standard Northern plains vocables.

Tempos. Moderate range for this style of song. There is no dancing during Flag Songs.

Dynamics and accents. Vocal dynamics remain at a level of *forte* throughout, and the drum is at *mezzo forte*, with no accents.

Tonality. The song is in E pentatonic (E, F♯, G♯, B, C♯) and the pitch is stable throughout.

Variation and ornamentation during performance. None.

Unusual characteristics. The drum plays a duple pattern while the melody is primarily in triple meter.

12. FLAG SONG

Wapaha Olowan

Native Thunder

12. Flag Song

13. RETREAT

Wowapi Glupapi

Description. Oglala Lakota Contemporary style word song, Native Thunder Singers, Pine Ridge Reservation, South Dakota. Performers are Jerome LeBeaux (head), Aaron Giago, Garfield Steele, Robert Brave Heart, Jenny Ghost Bear, Foster Cournoyer, Virgil Poafpybitty, Tyson Shay, and Jermaine Bell.
 Date. Recorded 5 May 2001 in Los Angeles. Transcribed September 2006.
 Bibliographic source. Previously unpublished, transcribed for this collection.
 Process. Transcribed by Tara Browner from a recorded performance of the Native Thunder Singers.
 Form. Length of song is eleven rounds plus a tail (coda) in an A-B-C form, which is standard in the style.
 Text. Lakota language text and Northern Plains vocables.
 Text translation as follows:

Oyate ki le lúta pe
he omani wacipeh lúta welo
he omani wacipeh lúta welo

([Indian] people the red way)
(they happy dancing red travel)
(they happy dancing red travel)
The Red Nation People follow the Red Road
Happily they follow the Red Road

Primary translation by Miles Whitecloud, Sioux Valley, Manitoba. Translation in parentheses by Tara Browner.
 Tempos. Moderate to accommodate dancers of many styles and ages, common in this type of song, with very little variation after a slight increase at the beginning of round 4.
 Dynamics and accents. Vocal dynamics remain at a level of *forte* throughout. As is standard with Northern Plains songs, dynamic variation is entirely within the drum part. A single player performs isolated accents, while the entire group renders larger changes in dynamic level.
 Tonality. The song is in A-flat pentatonic (A♭, B♭, C, E♭, F) throughout.
 Variation and ornamentation during performance. Melodic variations are found in the solo opening statement of each round as is usual in this style. Occasional extra-musical utterances by singers are marked with "x"-shaped note heads.
 Unusual characteristics. None.

Wowapi Glupapi

13. RETREAT

Wowapi Glupapi

Native Thunder

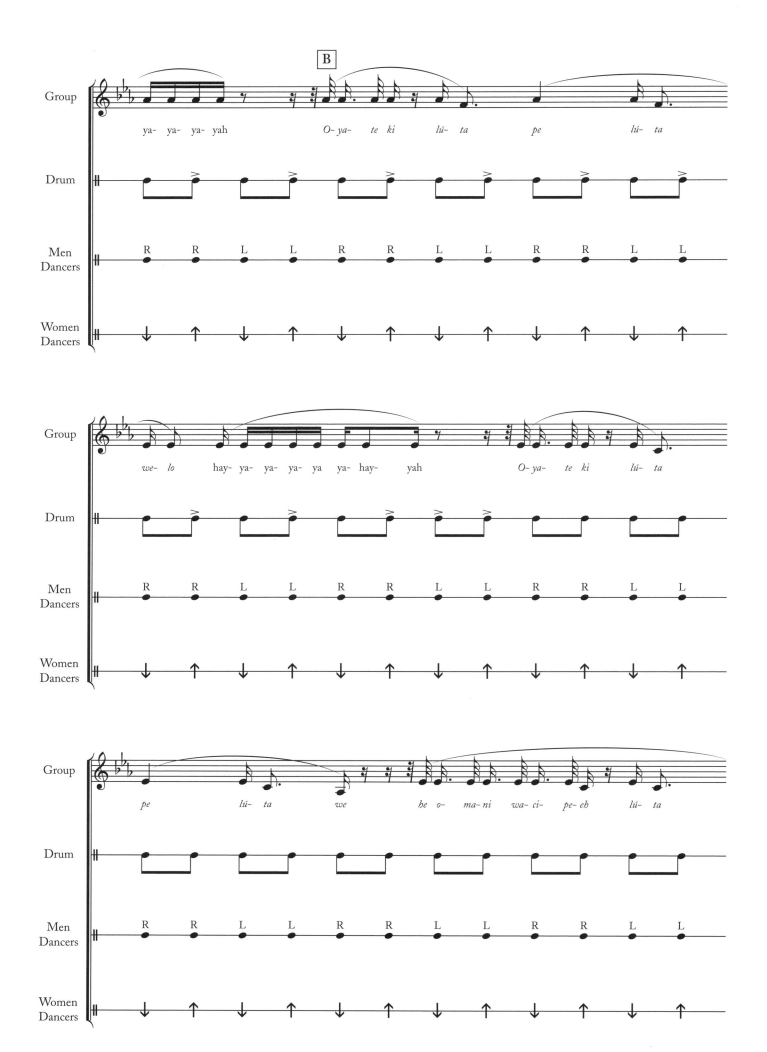

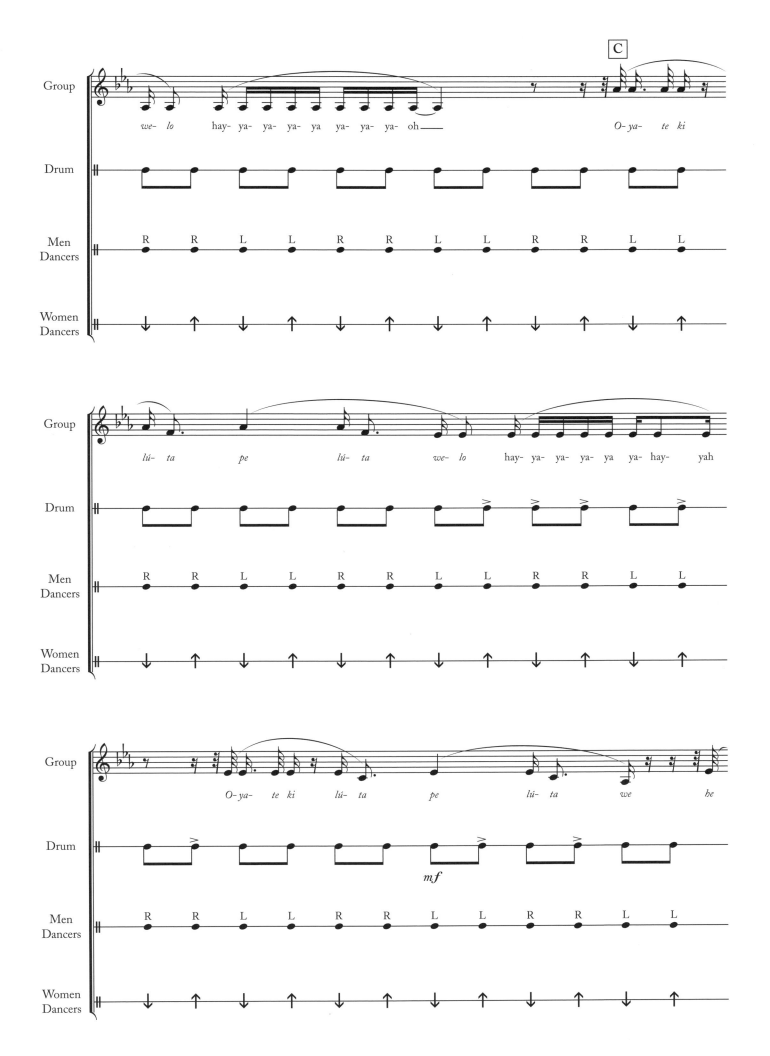

13. Retreat

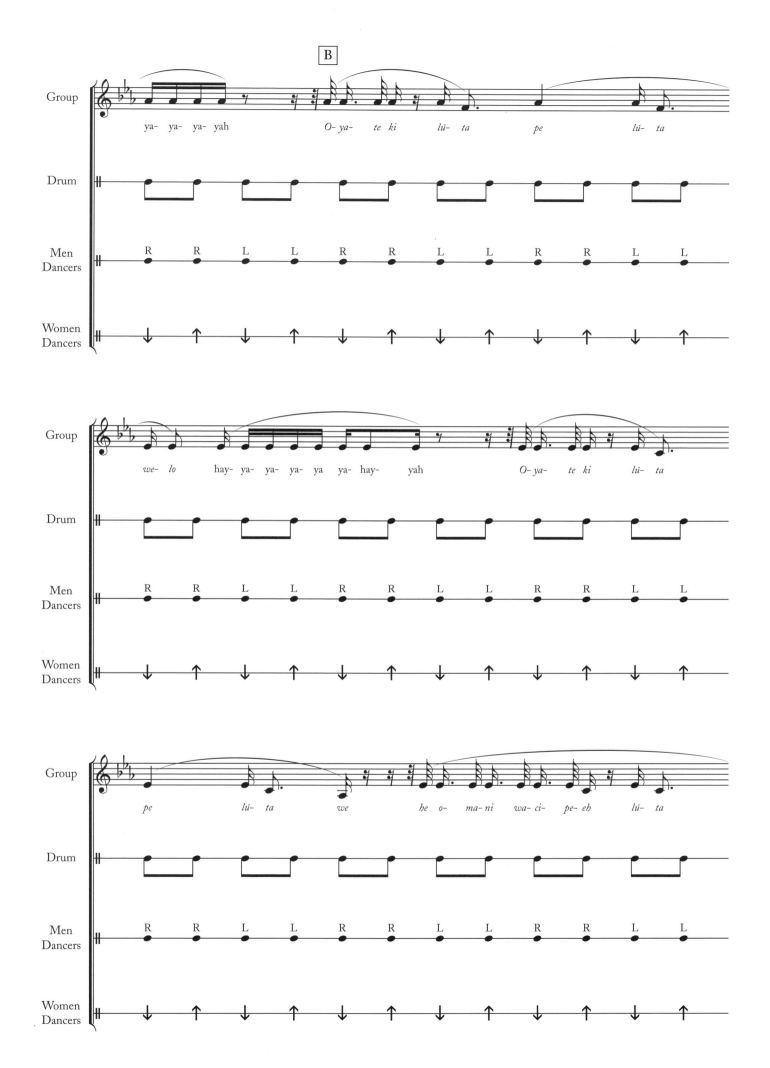

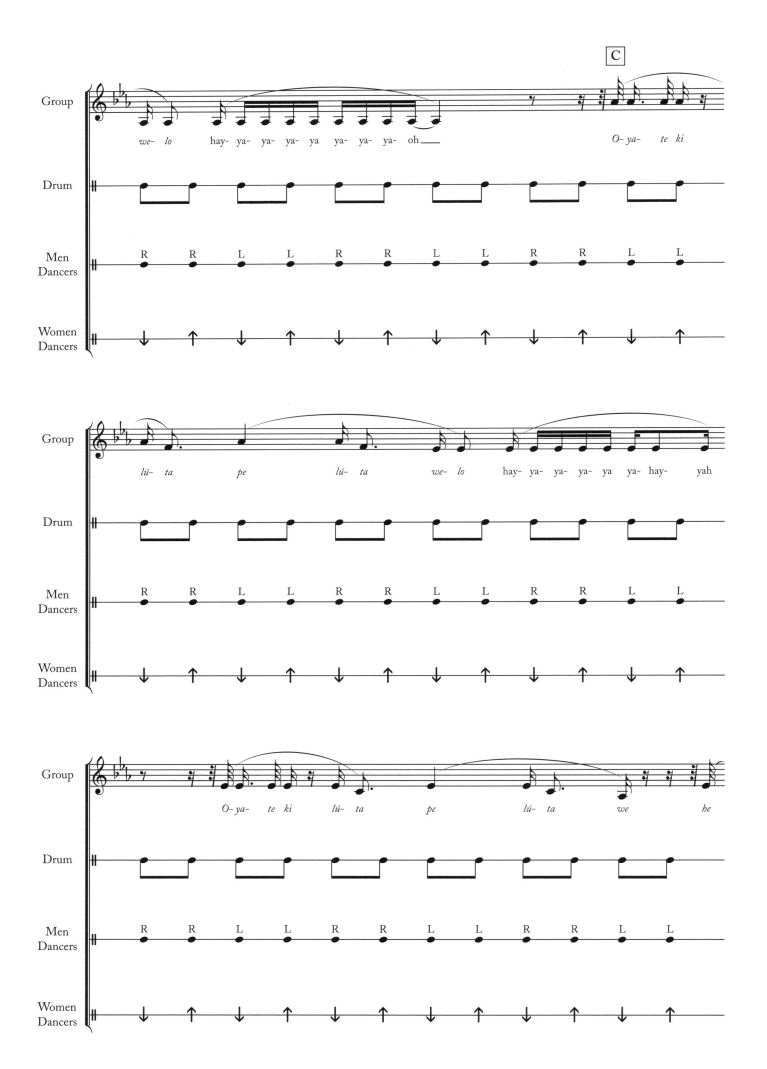

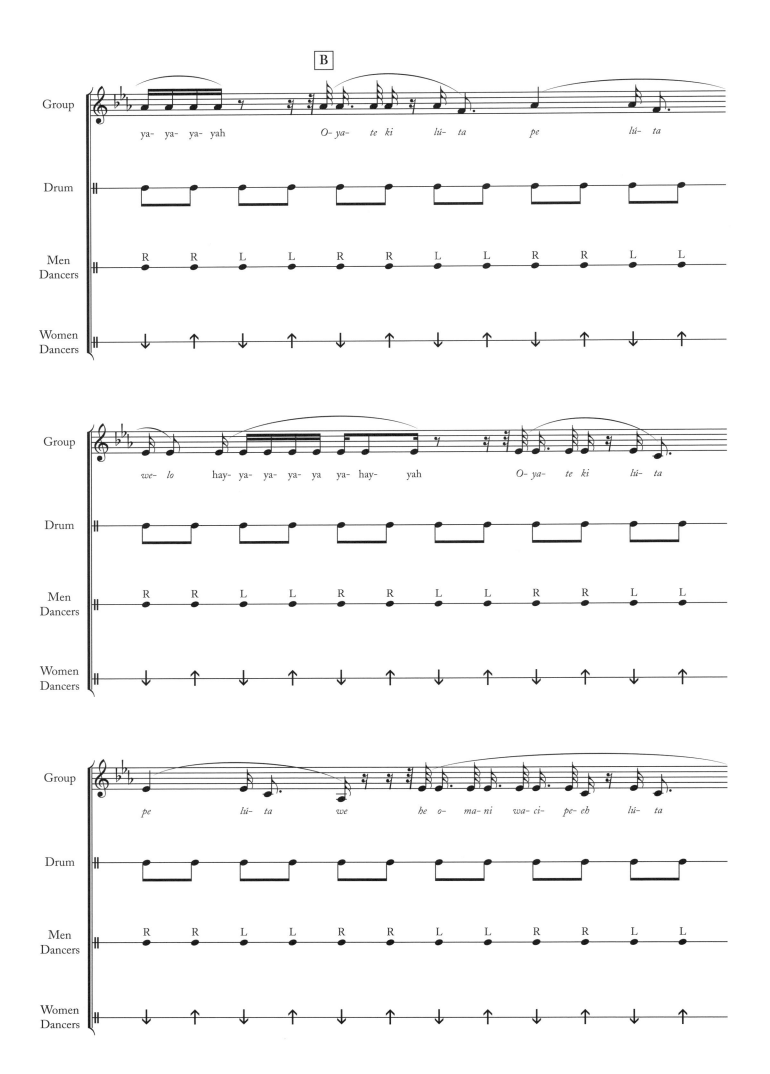

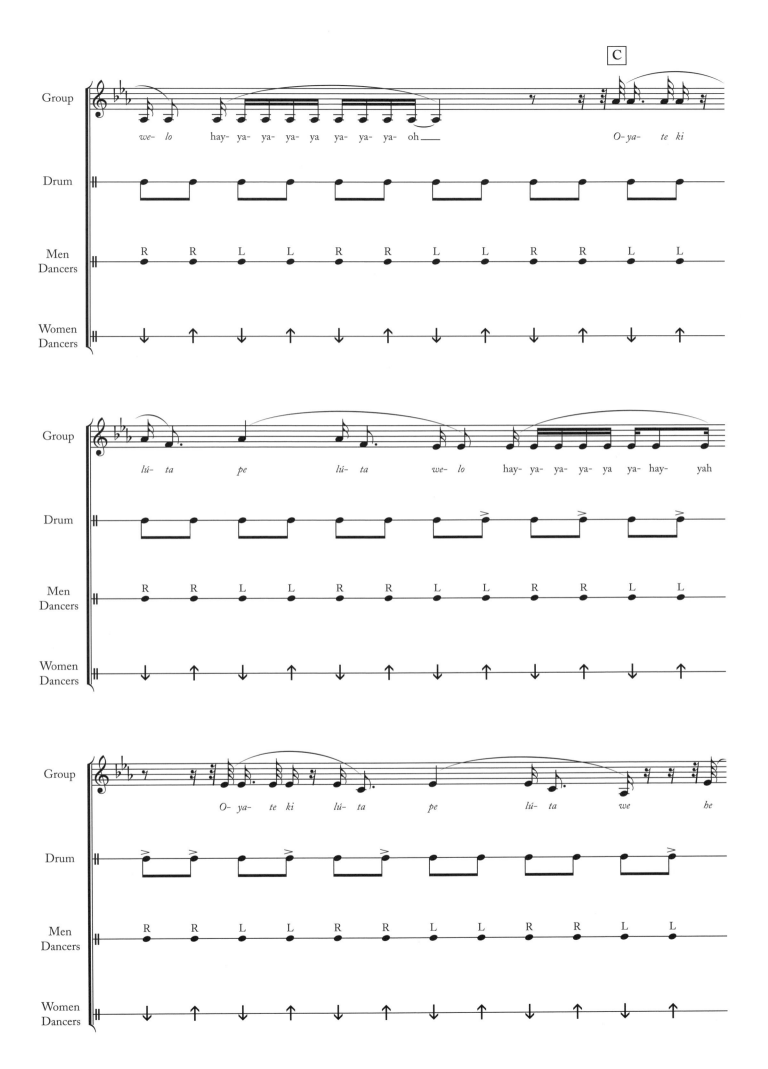

13. Retreat

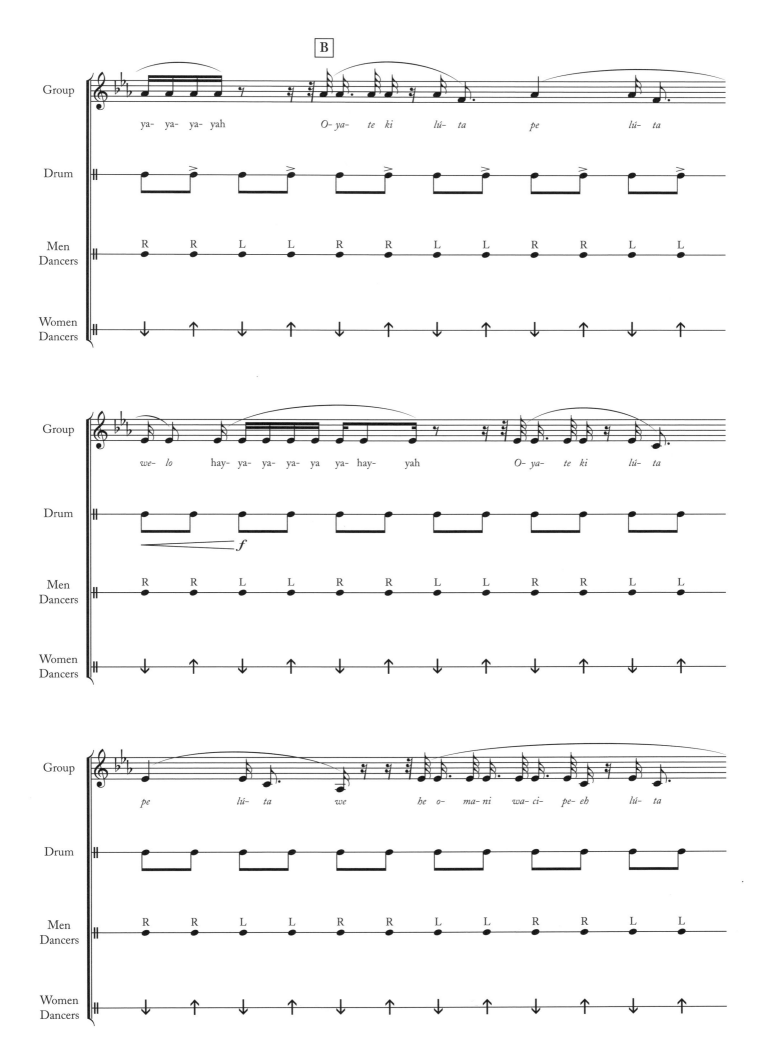

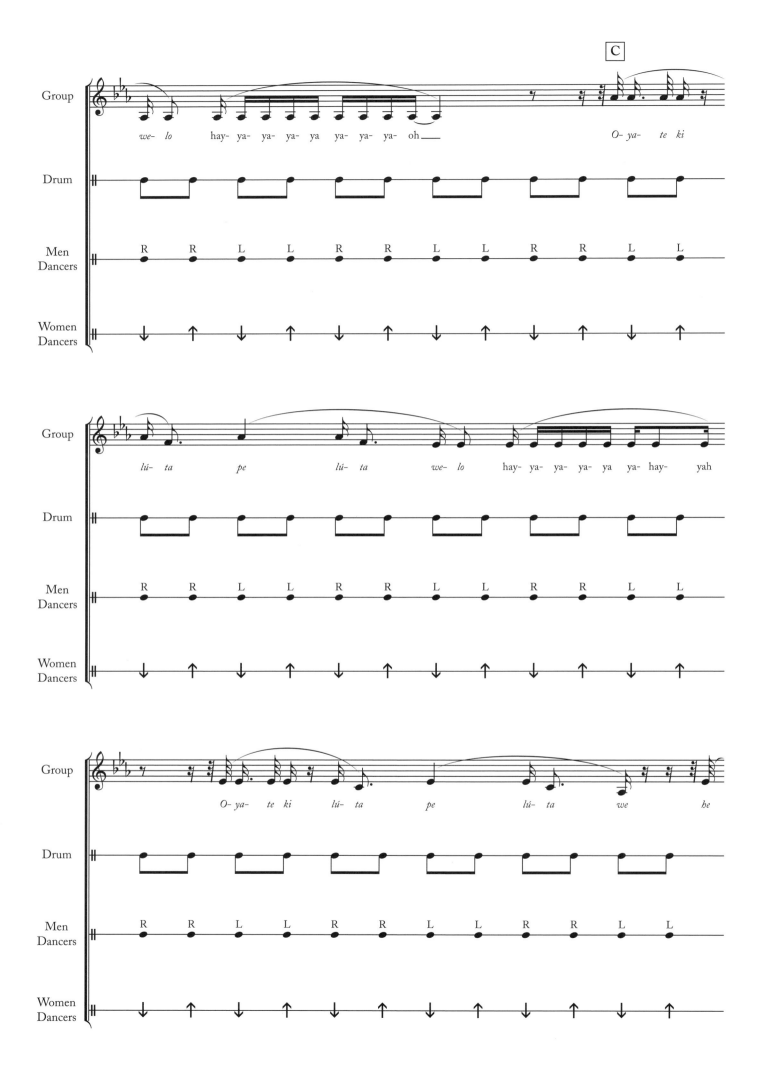

13. Retreat

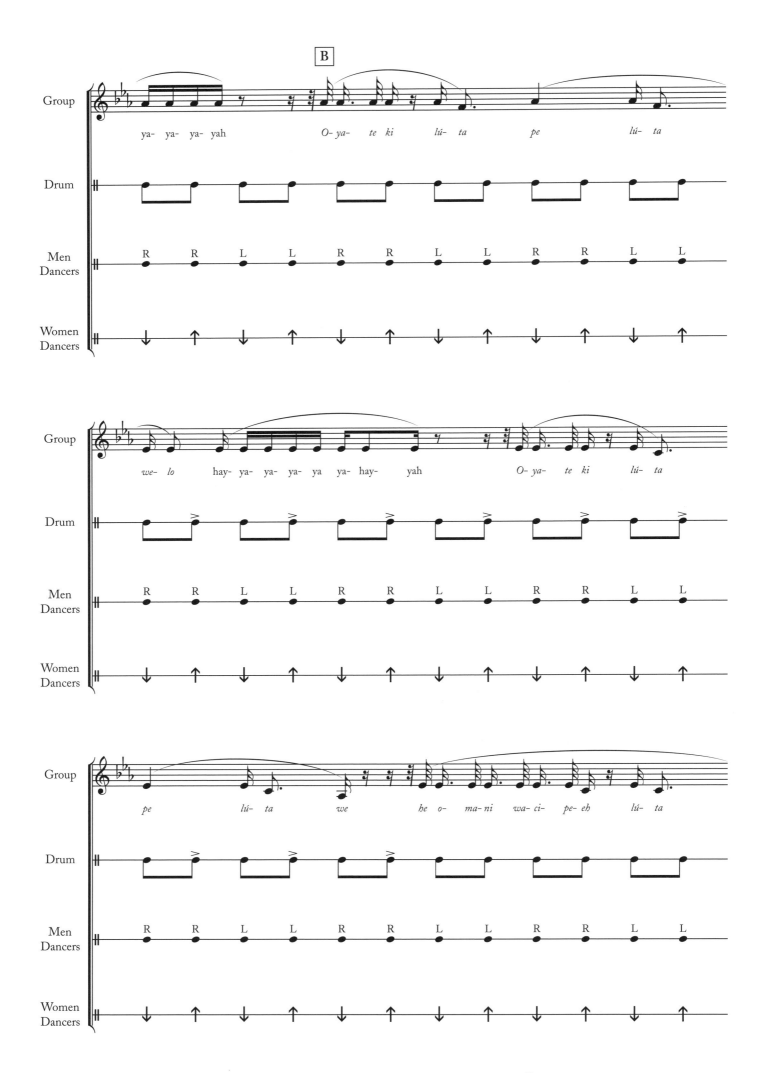

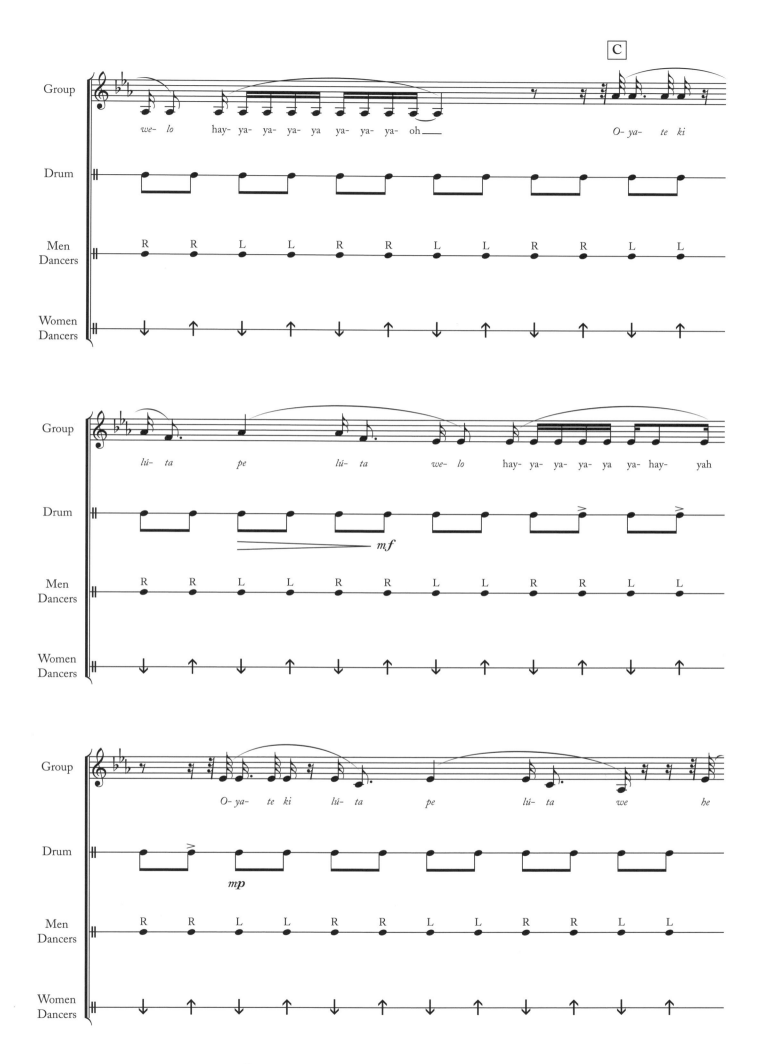

13. Retreat

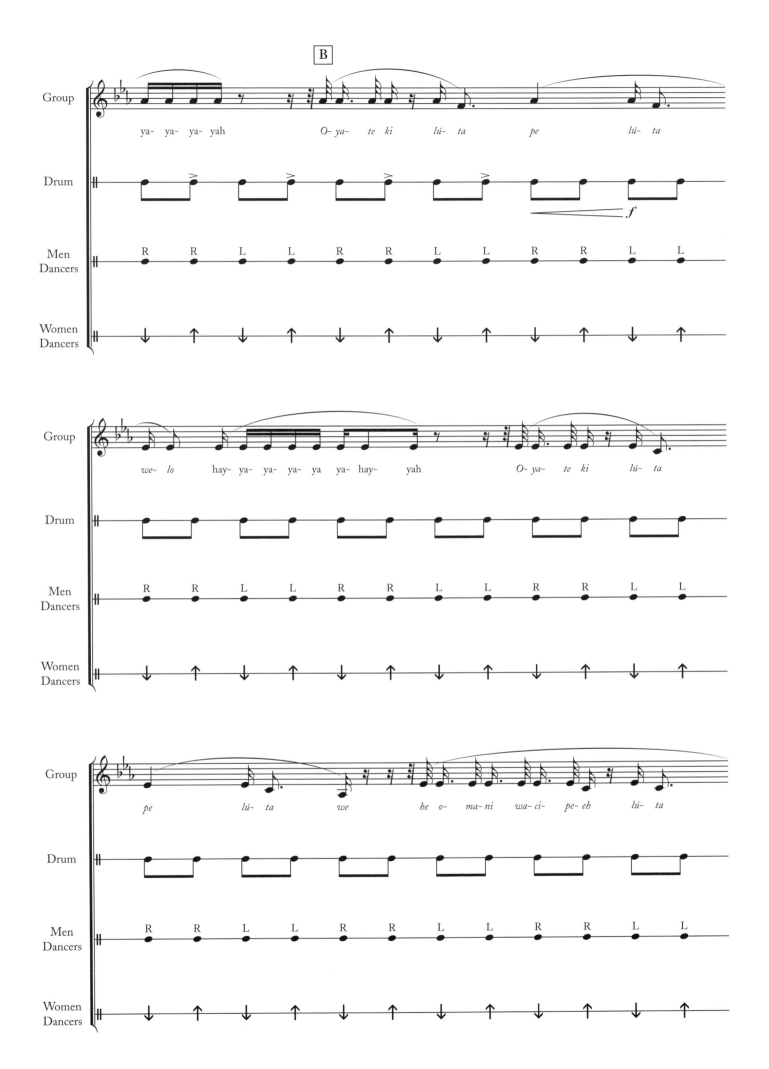

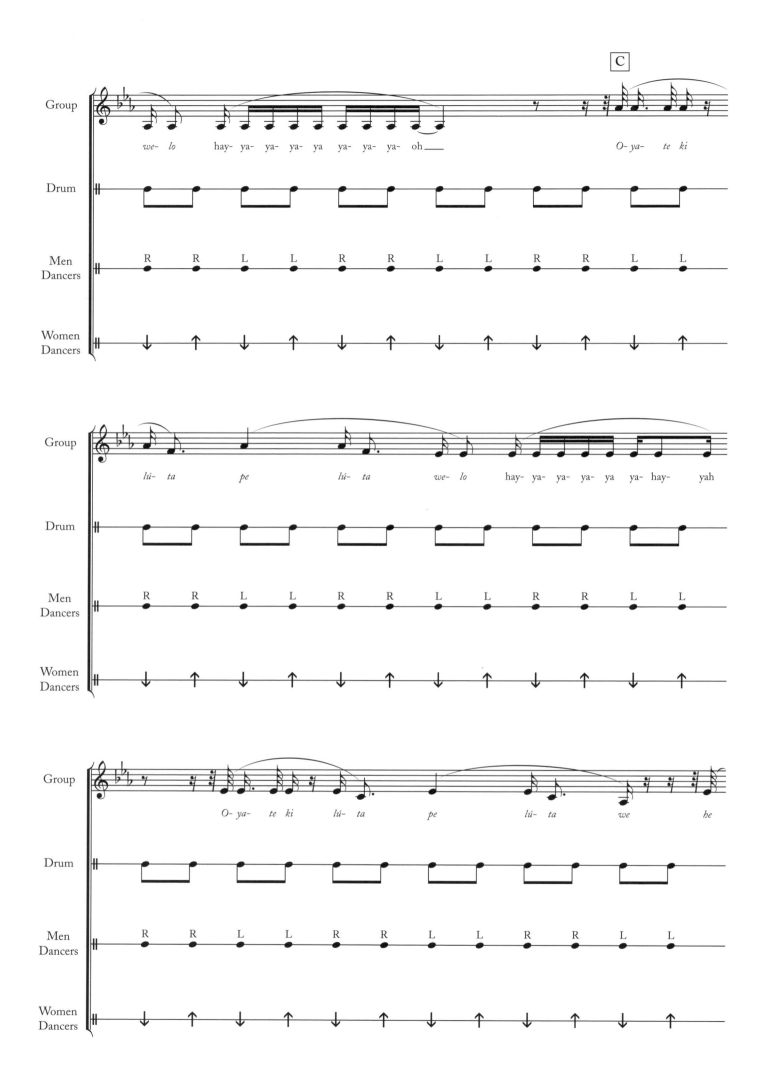

13. Retreat

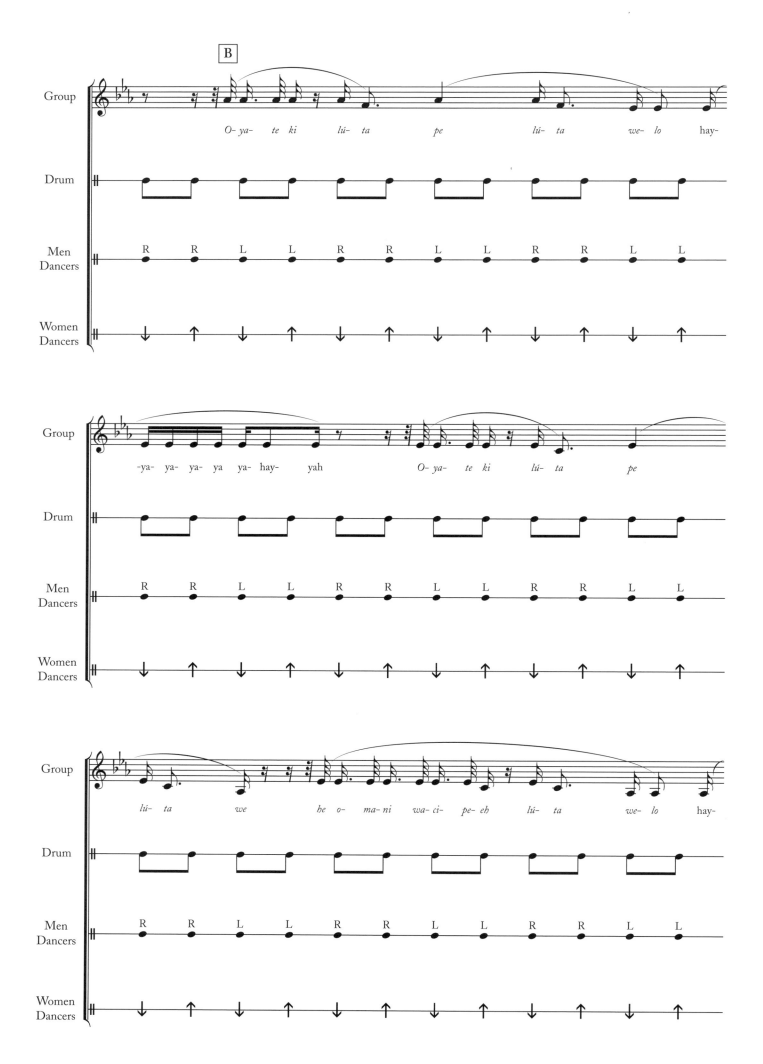

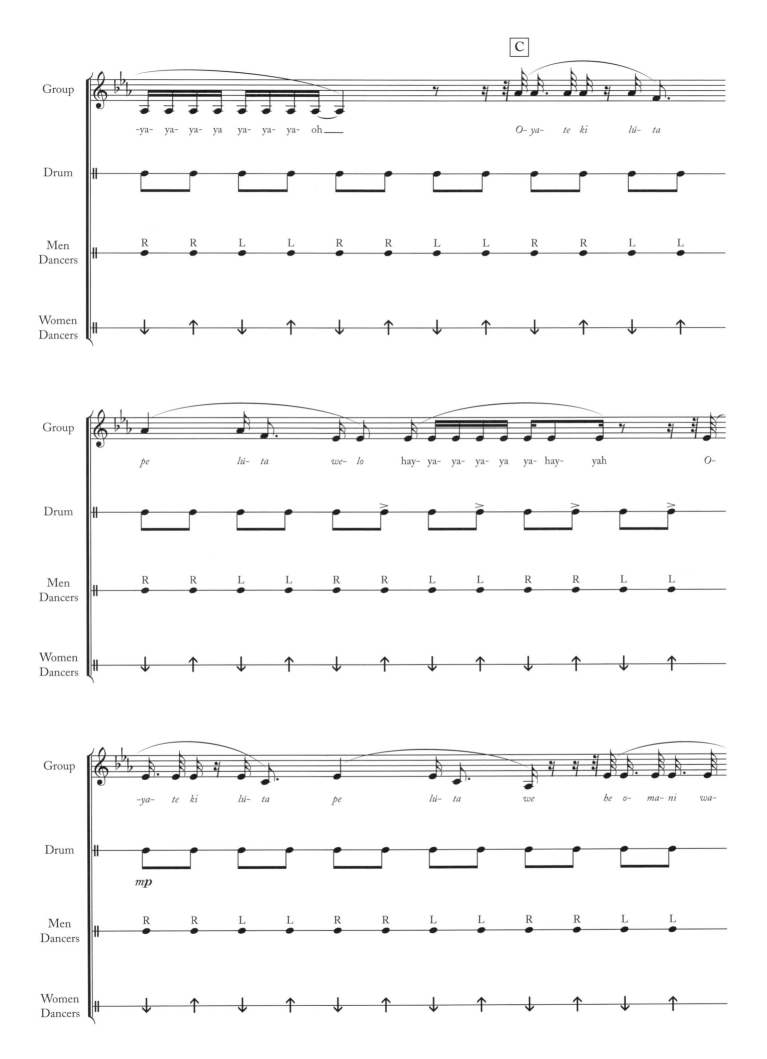

13. Retreat

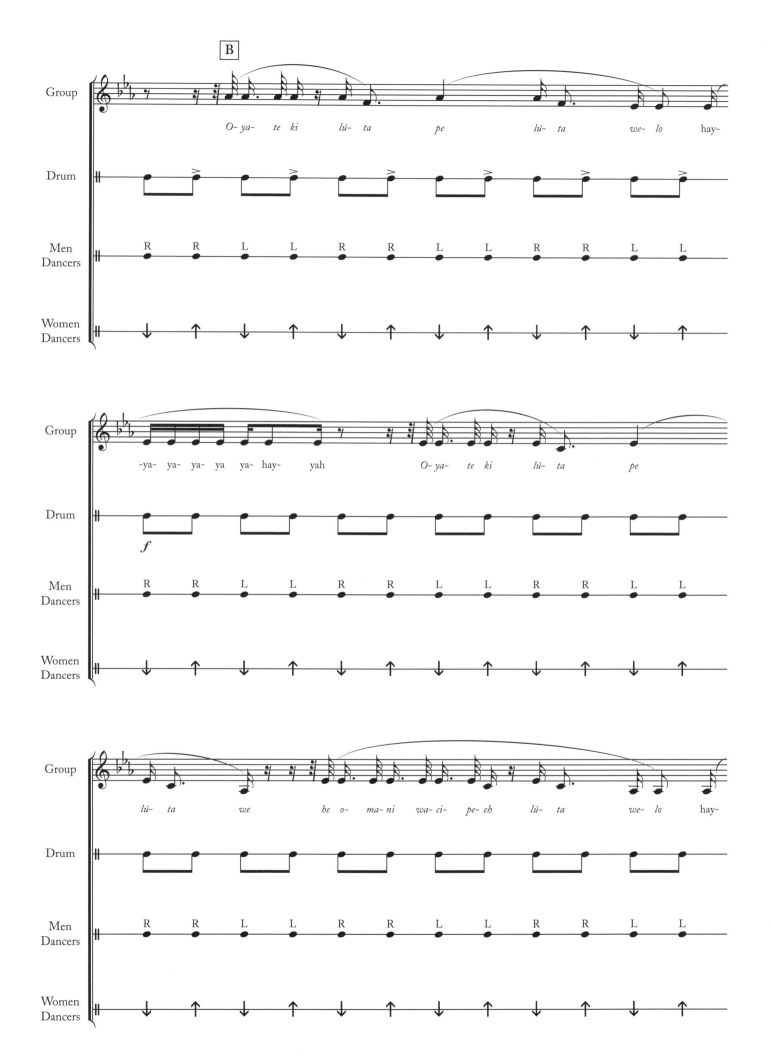

13. Retreat

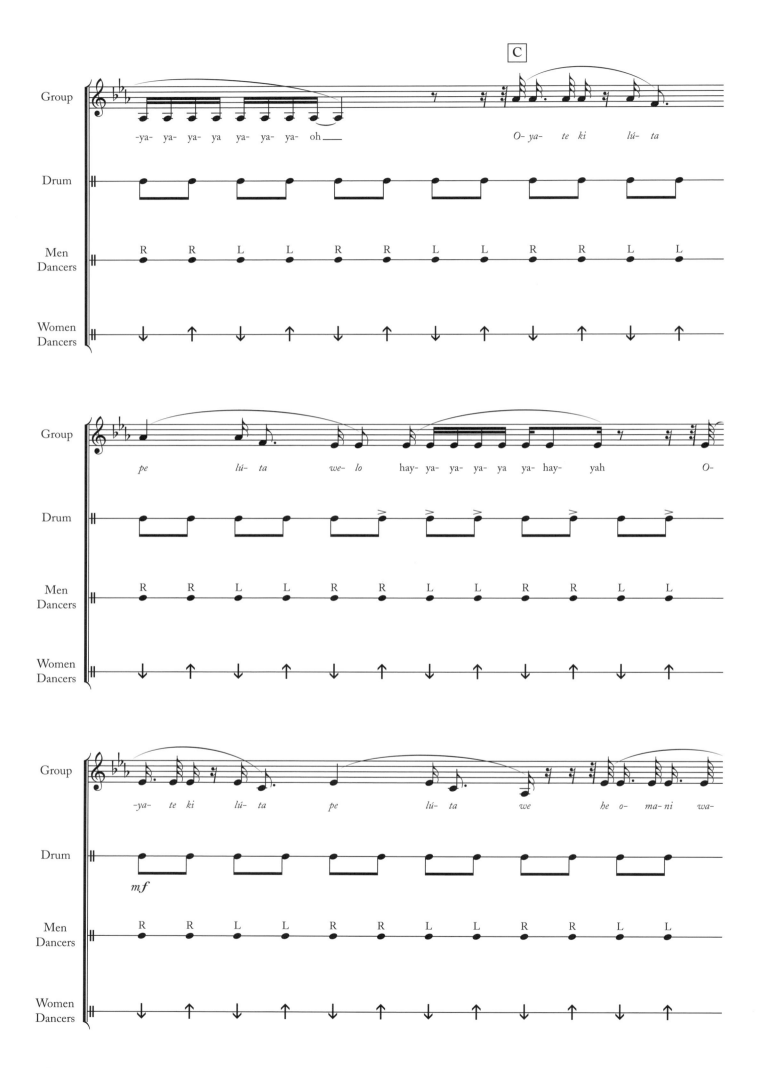

13. Retreat

13. Retreat

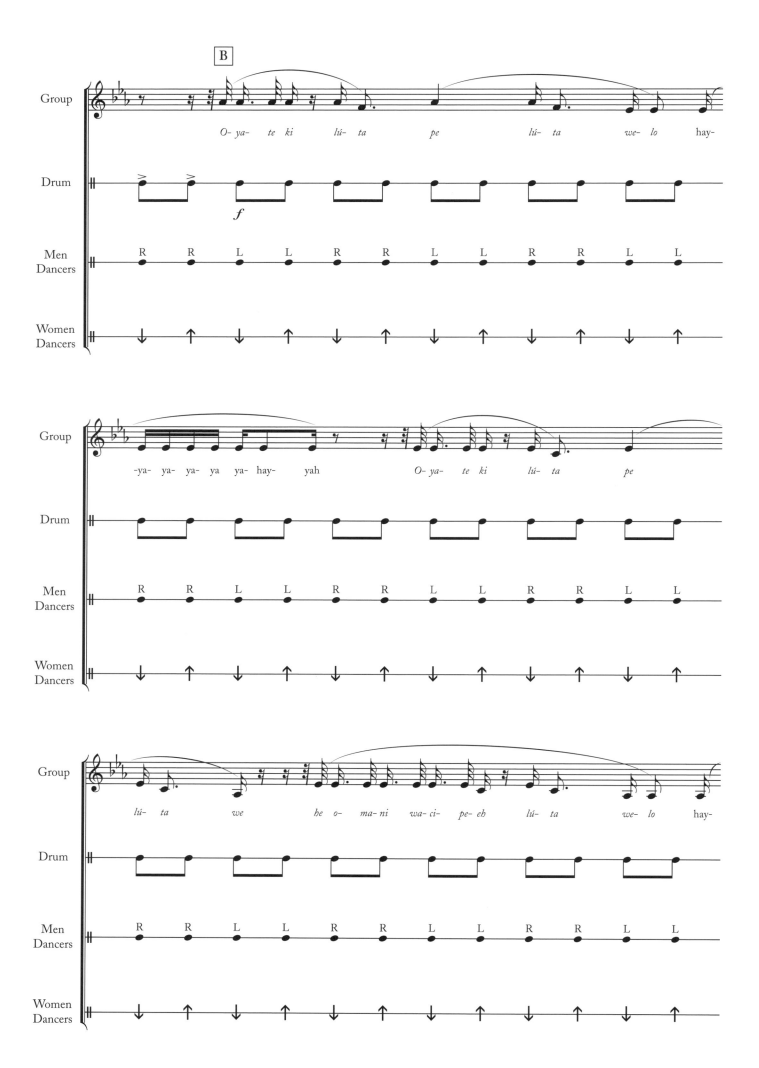

13. Retreat

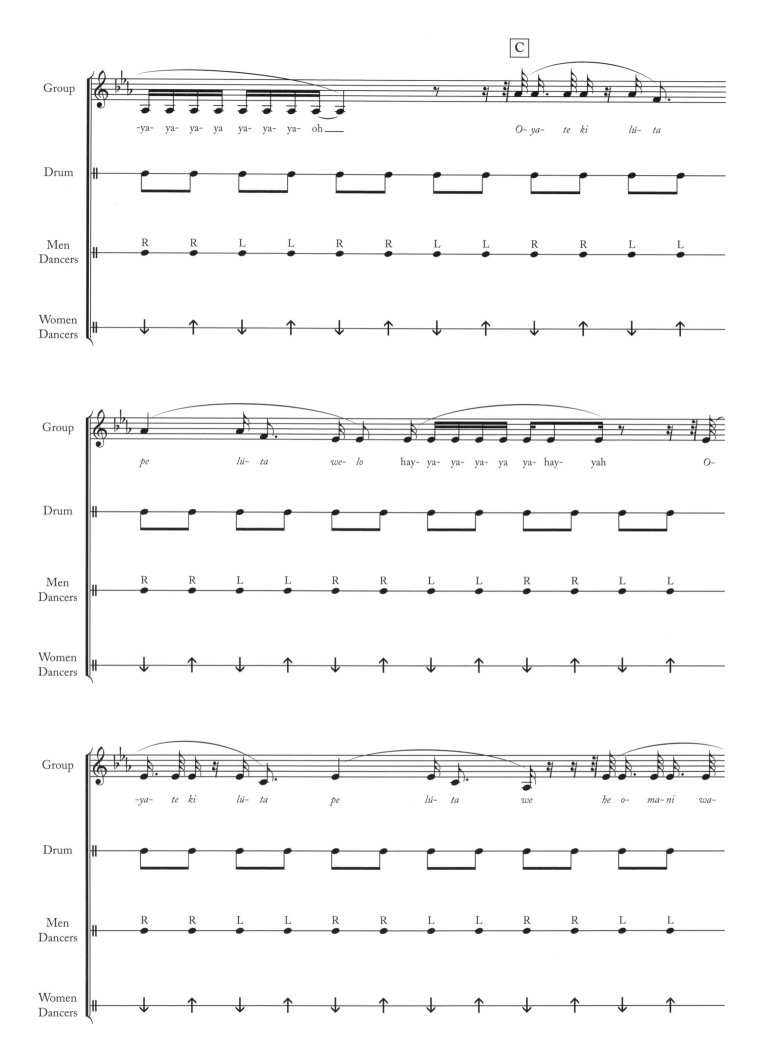

13. Retreat

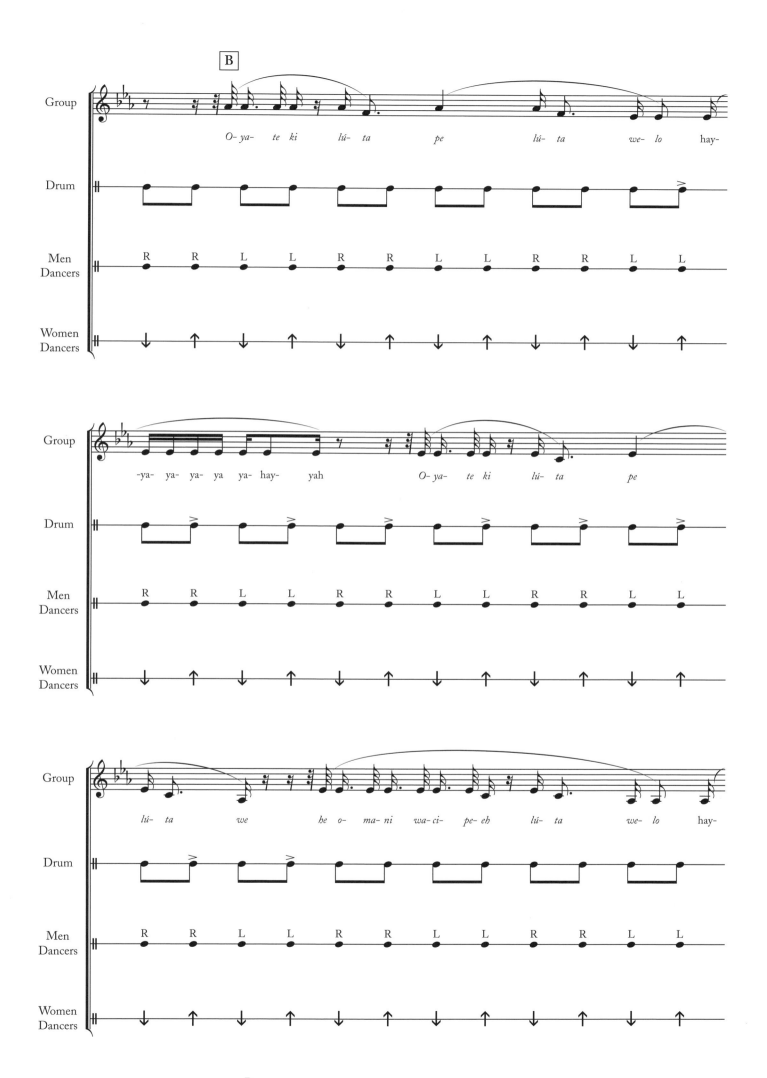

13. Retreat

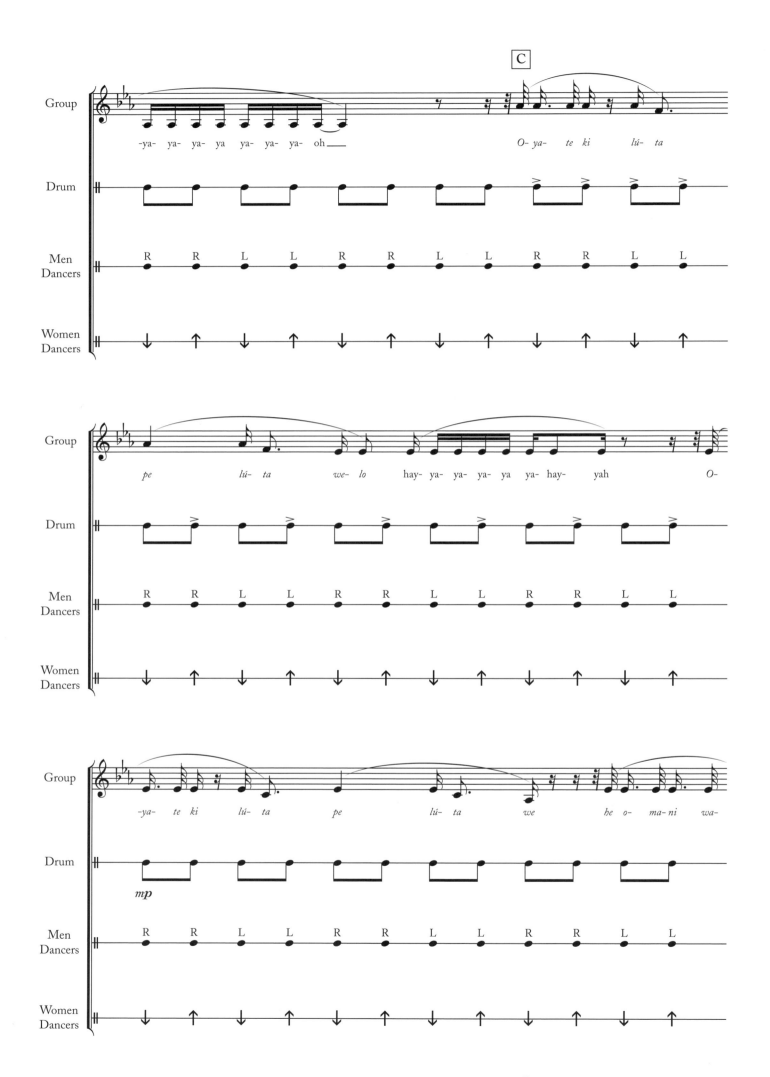

13. Retreat

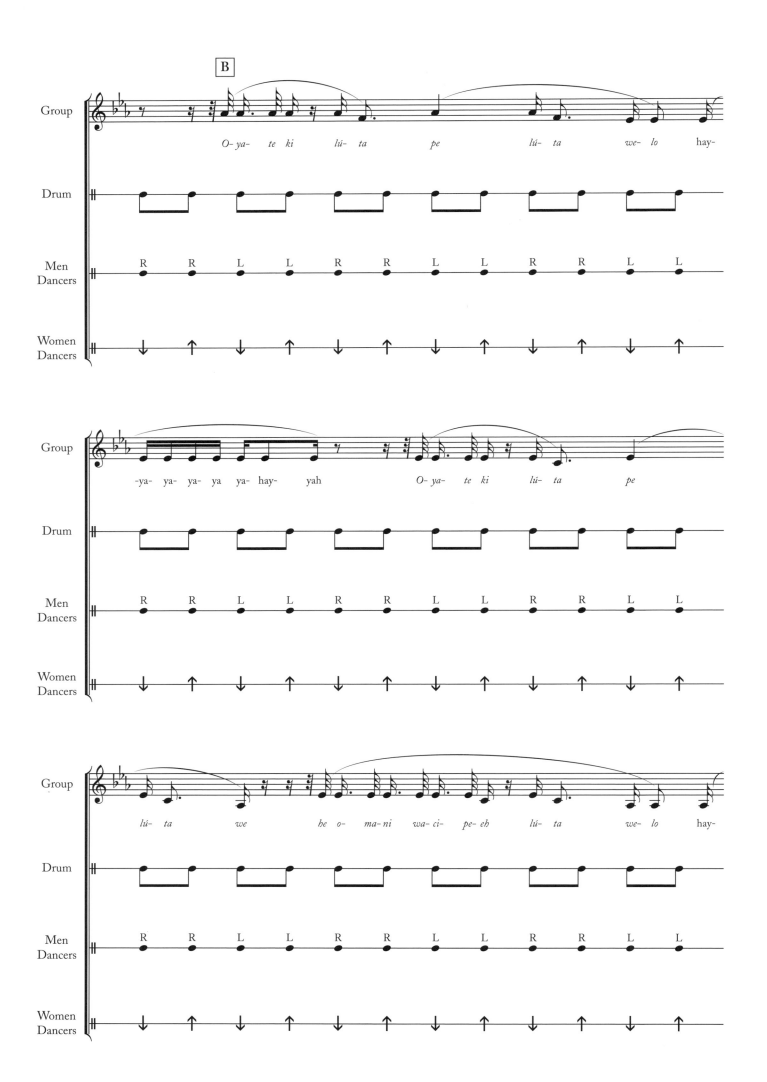

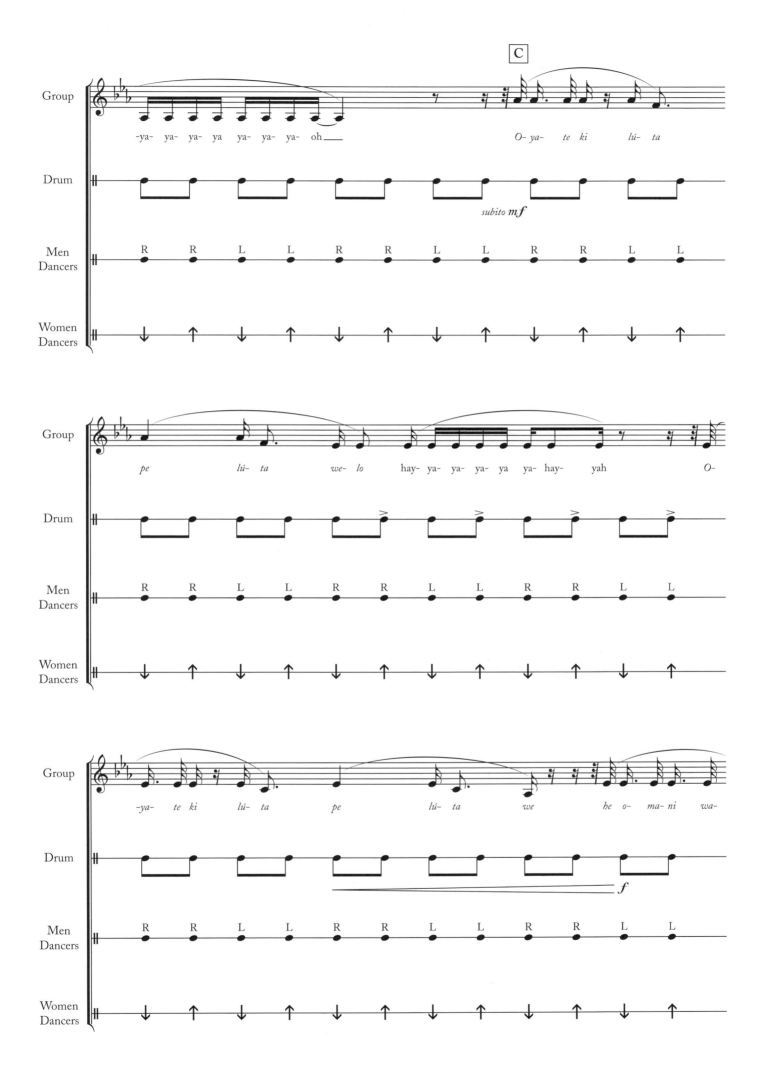

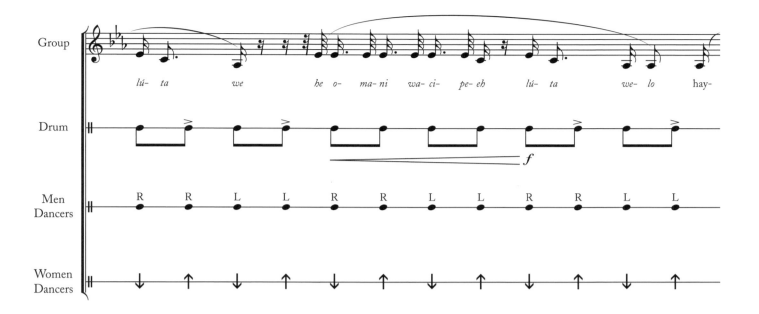
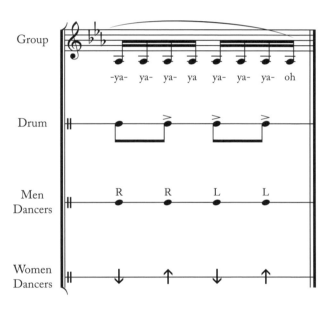

13. Retreat

APPARATUS

Sources

The recordings used for the individual transcriptions printed in this edition were made 5 May 2001 in Los Angeles, California, under the supervision of Tara Browner (field researcher and editor of this edition) at the annual pow-wow sponsored by the American Indian Student Association at the University of California, Los Angeles. Two Drum groups—Native Thunder (Northern) and the Cedartree Singers (Southern)—were chosen to record, based upon the ability of the researcher to obtain human subjects exemptions from the University of California, Los Angeles, Office for the Protection of Research Subjects, and more specifically, from the North General Institutional Review Board (NGIRB). These drum groups, because they were invited to the pow-wow as "Host Drums," could be contacted in advance of the event and listed in the exemption application. Other Drum groups were also at the pow-wow but could not be recorded due to the IRB restrictions. These groups were the Sooner Nation (Los Angeles), Wildhorse Singers (Los Angeles), Valley of the Sun (Tempe, Arizona), Desert Rumble (Indio, California), and the Red Horse Singers (Pine Ridge, South Dakota).

The two Drums recorded were the The Cedartree Singers of Falls Church, Virginia, and the Native Thunder Singers of the Pine Ridge Reservation in South Dakota.

Performers in the Cedartree Singers were Michael Rose (Cherokee), John Mark Rose (Cherokee), Jeff Bailey (Oglala/Sac and Fox), Erny Zah (Navajo), Jody Cummings (Lumbee/Cohaire), Vernell Capitan (Diné Nation), William A. Sebastian (Ojibway/Cayuga), William Clark (Cherokee), and Echohawk Neconie (Kiowa/Pawnee/Otoe).

Performers in the Native Thunder Singers were Jerome LeBeaux (Oglala Lakota), Aaron Giago (Oglala/Diné), Garfield Steele (Oglala Lakota), Robert Brave Heart Jr. (Lakota/Cheyenne), Jenny Ghost Bear (Oglala Lakota/Hunkpapa), Foster Cournoyer (Hunkpapa Sioux), Virgil Poafpybitty (Lakota/Kiowa/Comanche), Mike Carlow (Oglala Lakota), Tyson Shay (Shoshone Bannok/Ute), and Jermaine Bell (Arapaho/Lakota). George Patton (Lakota), a UCLA student, sat in with the group on some songs.

Selection Criteria

The decision was made before the event to record the first afternoon session of the pow-wow, in large part because that is typically when the singers are in their best voices, and also because the first session usually has a representative variety of songs. In addition, due to the field researcher (Tara Browner) sponsoring a Memorial Dance competition in honor of a deceased family member during the Saturday evening session, human subjects exemptions could only be obtained for the first afternoon session, because once a researcher begins to participate in an event, exemptions from human subjects protocols cannot be granted.

Recording began at 1:12 p.m. and finished at 5:17 p.m., a period that spanned the entire first session of the event from Grand Entry through the Retreat. During that time a total of thirteen songs, sung by the two Host Drum groups, were recorded by student assistants (Brandon Esten and Dennis Moristo) on small Sony hand-held cassette machines placed close to the singers. The recorders were high-quality but not digital or stereo, and they were chosen specifically because the groups were assured that no recordings made would be of a quality that might be professionally released and thus compete with their own commercial recordings. A total of fifty-eight minutes and eighteen seconds of singing was recorded. These recordings were then digitized using Sound Forge software and transferred to compact disc format by Jonathan Ritter, at the time a graduate student in the UCLA Ethnomusicology program. During the digitization process, some tape hiss and ambient noise was removed from the master recordings; otherwise they were unchanged, and remain of "field recording" quality.

Transcription Method

The actual transcriptions were done entirely by Tara Browner, using an A440 tuning fork as an initial pitch reference, and an electronic Seiko metronome to determine tempos. Complete melodic lines were double-checked against a Radio Shack MIDI keyboard after each round was roughed out, and occasionally a hand held Korg tuner was used to determine whether or not pitches should be notated with an added symbol designating sharpness (see below). Because the transcriptions were set into professional notation using Finale 2007 music writing software, they could also be played back in MIDI form on a Macintosh computer and checked again against the field recording, although this was done primarily to check rhythms. Rhythms were transcribed first, and then the pitches of the vocal lines were worked out.

With the drum patterns a constant in each song, these patterns could also work as a stable point of reference against which rhythms could be notated. Once it was decided that the drum patterns would be set in paired eighth-notes beamed to match the footwork of the male dancers (which is right-right/left-left), "check pattern" sheets were created of evenly spaced sixteenth notes using Finale, with the first and third sixteenth notes of each barred grouping lining up with the first and second eighth notes of each eighth-note pair in the drum score. This allowed the rhythms of the melodic line to be layered over the sixteenth-note check pattern, using the phrasing unique to the melody. Example 3 shows a section of check pattern with the melodic rhythm laid out on top of it.

This initial transcription of the rhythm became the basis for the next part of the process, which was to transcribe the pitches of the melody. Because each song was performed in a series of relatively identical "rounds," initially only the first or second round was transcribed in order to be used as a template for the later realization of each complete song. After the melody had been transcribed, vocables and/or Native language text was added to the melodic part (which at this stage was roughly hand-written over an eighth-note drum pattern), and files of texts were created in Microsoft Word for transfer into Finale.

When rhythm check pattern sheets, melodic transcriptions, and text files were complete, they were turned over to Benjamin Harbert, a graduate student assistant (and professional Finale typesetter), to be collated into a single document using Finale 2007. This was an exacting process, because the rhythms and phrasing of the melody needed to be placed exactly over the repeating eighth-note pattern of the drum score that would be in the final version of the transcription but frequently did not coincide with

EXAMPLE 3. Check pattern with melodic rhythm.

EXAMPLE 4.

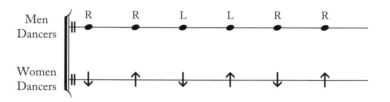

what the software judged to be a natural phrasing. After the parts of the transcription had been layered into a single document, they were passed back and forth electronically for corrections, often as many as seven or eight times; each round was then printed up and such elements as phrase marks, tempos, accents, and dynamics were manually added by Browner, and adjustments were made to the melodic line and occasional non-melodic vocalizations. Dance scores were also added at this time, based upon field notes taken at the time of the recording. The layout of the dance scores initially was conceptualized by Browner but fine-tuned by Harbert, who also contributed the idea of having the Head Singer's vocal lines phase in and out of the score. The last part of the process involved Harbert collating all of the individual rounds into the final transcription of a complete song performance.

Editorial Markings

Section Marking Scheme

Pow-wow songs are repetitive and cyclic, with each cycle commonly being referred to as a "round" by Native participants (the terms "push-up" or "set" are also sometimes used). For labeling purposes in this edition, each cycle through the song is referred to as a Round, with cycles after the first round numbered as "Round 2, Round 3 . . ." and so on. Often songs have a short coda at the end, after a full stop (written as a fermata), and these are labeled "Tails," which is also the appropriate Native term, and comes for the historic practice of a designated "Tail Dancer" being the only individual allowed to dance during this final coda.

Numbering within rounds was a more complex issue, and it was ultimately decided to use the same style of lettering (A, B, C . . .) that is commonly used in scores of Western music, rather than use letters that correspond with an analysis of formal structure. This determination was based upon the fact that these transcriptions are intended for a critical musical edition, and not a text devoted to large-scale examinations of musical form. This means that, rather than the repetitive parts of a round being designated with identical letters followed by different numbers, each large section within a round was given a new letter. A few of the songs with unusual numbers of discrete phrases within sections have the phrases marked with numbers after the main section letter, for example, B1, B2, B3. But when that section repeats *within* a round after a major cadence (and almost all of them do), the return is marked as C1, C2, C3, etc.

The Dance Score

The dance score (see example 4) is a graphic representation of the footwork of the male and female traditional dancers, as it relates to the drum part of each song. The "r" and "l" in the men's part signify the right and left feet, while the arrows in the women's part correspond to the movement of the dancer's legs up and down as they step forward.

Accidentals

Accidentals introduced into the score are good until cancelled.

Dynamics

Dynamics were established at the time of the initial performance, and based upon the principle of the vocal part always being at the level of *forte*. Because in live performance the sound level of the singers is unchanging, and dynamic changes are made by means of drum playing, all dynamic markings are in relationship to the assumption of a steady dynamic level in the vocal part.

Pitches

Pitches correspond with those of the traditional Western diatonic scale, with the exception of some tones that were approximately one-quarter of a tone sharp. These tones are marked with a + sign over the note.

Tempo

Tempos are figured at the rate of a quarter note (or dotted quarter note) equaling each full metronome beat. These were carefully determined using an electronic metronome, and often shift back and forth abruptly within the space of a few beats, especially in transitional sections of songs in the Southern War Dance style.

Time Signatures

Although there is a concept of meter (duple and triple) in the drum parts of pow-wow songs, it connects to the dancing, and not the phrasing of the vocal parts, with the exception of cadential phrases. In order to preserve this aesthetic, which is based upon the spiritual belief that the drum is a living being with a voice separate from that of the singers, time signatures are not used.

Notation

Stemming, beaming, ties, and other notational conventions. Other than the specialized notational elements discussed below (and sampled in example 5), the notation follows standard conventions regarding stems and ties. For clarity and to allow space for dynamic markings, the drum part is always written with the stems down. Beaming of pitches in the vocal lines, however, is entirely separate from the beaming of the drum

EXAMPLE 5. Specialized notational elements.

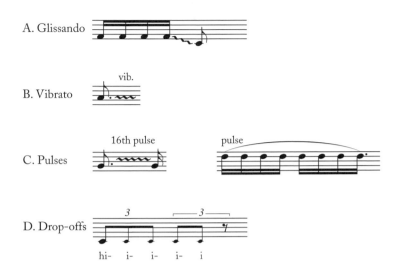

part, because the two parts operate in separate musical realms, coinciding only at cadences. Separate beaming, combined with phrase marking, uses the notation as a graphic representation of this disconnection.

Glissandos. Glissandos are descending glides downward that begin and end on specific pitches as marked.

Vibrato. Vibrato is a non-metrical oscillation between the pitch marked and the semi-tone above it.

Pulses. A pulse is defined as a vocal waver that does not change pitch but instead consists of a series of repeating pulsating tones, with a very slight emphasis on each in a way that sounds metrical. There is no separation or articulation between tones, and a pulse is always on a single drawn-out syllable. The sound is a result of a large group performance, and the notation approximates what is heard by the audience when multiple singers with heavy conflicting vibratos articulate a long tone. Pulses are marked in a number of ways, but always with the term "pulse."

Grace notes. Grace notes are always articulated before the beat.

Drop-offs. A drop-off marks a moment when all the singers articulate the first pitch in a grouping and then the pitches that follow are sung by only one or two singers. It is different from a *subito decrescendo* in that there is a thinning of the vocal texture.

Articulation

Accent marks. Accent marks indicate an attack one dynamic level above that which is written in the score at any given point.

Legato marks. Legato marks (only in the vocal part) indicate a slurring together of pitches, with a retention of the overall rhythmic framework and a distinctive articulation of the vocal part.

Staccato marks. Staccato marks over notes designate a clipped vocal attack and percussive articulation of the corresponding vocable or word.

Fermatas

A fermata indicates an extended pause (usually about five seconds) but not an extension of the pitch. The dancers pause in place.

TABLE 1. Phonetic key.

Pawnee		Lakota/Nakota		Vocables	
a	as in father	s	as in shoe	a	as in father (includes hah, yah, ah, wah)
i	as in field	c	as in church	ay	as in angel (includes hay, way, yay)
ii	as in field	k	as in key	ee	as in see
n	as in sing	j	as in déjà vu*	i	as in high (includes hi)
		a	as in father	oi	as in oil
		i	as in field	oh	as in toe (includes ho, hoh, yo, yoh)
		o	as in hoe	ow	as in hour
		e	as in they	uh	as in unusual

* Term recommended by a linguist—this "J" sound does not exist in English.

Phrase Arcs

Phrase arcs appearing over the vocal line indicate that part of the line that is being sung in one breath (at least by the majority of singers).

Text

Native language. Sections of song texts in Native American languages are always in italics. Spellings in Pawnee are standardized according to the versions used by the American Indian Studies Research Institute at Indiana University. Spellings in Lakota and Nakota are those given by the singers, as the orthography of these languages is not completely standardized.

Vocables. Sections of song texts in vocables are always in plain text.

Phonetic key. See table 1.

Critical Commentary

Critical commentaries, including recording histories (if documented), texts and their English translations, observations on tonality, and a sketching out of formal structures, precede each song.

LITERATURE CITED

Agawu, Kofi. "The Invention of 'African Rhythm'." *Journal of the American Musicological Society* 48, no. 2 (1995): 380–95.

Browner, Tara. *Heartbeat of the People: Music and Dance of the Northern Pow-wow.* Urbana and Chicago: University of Illinois Press, 2002.

Crawford, Richard. *America's Musical Life: A History*. New York: W.W. Norton & Company, 2001.

Densmore, Frances. "The Study of Indian Music." *Musical Quarterly* 1, no. 2 (1915): 187–97.

———. *Teton Sioux Music*. Bureau of American Ethnology Bulletin 61. Washington, D.C.: Smithsonian Institution, 1918.

Ellingson, Ter. "Transcription." In *Ethnomusicology: An Introduction*, ed. Helen Myers, 110–52. New York and London: W.W. Norton & Company, 1992.

———. "Notation." In *Ethnomusicology: An Introduction*, ed. Helen Myers, 153–64. New York and London: W.W. Norton & Company, 1992.

Finnegan, Ruth H. *The Hidden Musicians: Music-making in an English Town*. Cambridge and New York: Cambridge University Press, 1989.

Guest, Ann Hutchinson. *Dance Notation: The Process of Recording Movement on Paper*. New York: Dance Horizons, 1984.

Hagedorn, Katherine. *Divine Utterances: The Performance of Afro-Cuban Santeria*. Washington D.C. : Smithsonian Institution Press, 2001.

Hood, Mantle. "The Challenge of 'Bi-Musicality'." *Ethnomusicology* 4, no. 2 (1960): 55–59.

Lindsay Levine, Victoria, ed. *Writing American Indian Music: Historic Transcriptions, Notations, and Arrangements*. Music of the United States of America 11. Middleton, Wisc.: A-R Editions, 2002.

Merriam, Alan. *Ethnomusicology of the Flathead Indians*. Viking Fund Publication in Anthropology, Number 44. New York: Wenner Gren Foundation, 1967.

Nettl, Bruno. *Music in Primitive Culture*. Cambridge, Mass., and London: Harvard University Press, 1956.

Powers, William. *War Dance: Plains Indian Musical Performance*. Tucson: University of Arizona Press, 1990.

Roberts, Helen H. "New Phases in the Study of Primitive Music." *American Anthropologist* 24, no. 2 (1922): 114–60.

Samuels, David William. *Putting a Song on Top of It: Expression and Identity on the San Carlos Apache Reservation*. Tucson: University of Arizona Press, 2004.

Seeger, Charles. "Prescriptive and Descriptive Music Writing." *Musical Quarterly* 44, no. 2 (1958): 184–95.

Yung, Bell, ed. *Celestial Airs of Antiquity: Music of the Seven-String Zither of China.* Recent Researches in the Oral Traditions of Music 5. Middleton, Wisc.: A-R Editions, 1997.

Vander, Judith. *Songprints: The Musical Experience of Five Shoshone Women.* Urbana and Chicago: University of Illinois Press, 1988.

Weibel-Orlando, Joan. *Indian Country L.A.: Maintaining Ethnic Community in a Complex Society.* Urbana and Chicago: University of Illinois Press, 1991.

Wissler, Clark. "General Discussion of Shamanistic and Dancing Societies." In *Anthropological Papers of the American Museum of Natural History* 11, no. 12 (1916): 853–76.

Wong, Deborah. *Speak it Louder: Asian Americans Making Music.* New York: Routledge, 2004.